Enchanted Whispers

WIT & WISDOM
from the Mouths of Babes
(& Momma Too)

by
Jean Lanahan

authorHOUSE™

1663 LIBERTY DRIVE, SUITE 200
BLOOMINGTON, INDIANA 47403
(800) 839-8640
WWW.AUTHORHOUSE.COM

[handwritten: Jackie]

[handwritten: To Lou 's Barb- For all you've done for us - Thanks ♥ Enjoy.]

[handwritten: Jean Lanahan]

[handwritten: Eliyabeth]

First published by AuthorHouse 10/24/2005

ISBN: 1-4208-7284-2 (sc)

Printed in the United States of America
Bloomington, Indiana

This book is printed on acid-free paper.

Comments from the "Hood". Parenthood that is!

"The most common things in every child's day are the miracles Jean Lanahan chronicles through the voices of her children. Enchanted Whispers tells us that there are no common things – each moment with a child is a gift from God, to be valued, appreciated and celebrated. Anyone who loves children and the things they say will read and reread this book for the jewels that come out of children's mouths. Authentic voices on every page!"

Debra Haskell, Educator; Principal, Ella F. Hoxie Elementary School, Sagamore Beach, MA

"I am a mother of two, a grandmother of one, a teacher of young children for more than 20 years, and I thoroughly enjoyed reading 'Momma Jeana's' awe-inspiring words. She truly captivates her audience, of young and old, with her telling of events from her young daughter's lives. Jean illustrates with her writing, the innocence and wonders of young children in their quest to understand and learn about their world. An easy, relaxing read for anyone to enjoy, and when done, all will have a smile on their face!"

Judy Tocci, Director, Rainbow Preschool, Sagamore Beach, MA

"Jean Lanahan puts pen, paper, and feelings into a witty, lighthearted, and truthful read that all mothers can relate to. This book lets you know that you're not alone going through the same wonderful joys (and the same trying moments) of parenthood. As a mother of four girls (ages 5 to 19), I am qualified to give Enchanted Whispers a five-star review!"

Michelle Oliver, Stay at Home Mom, Bourne, MA

"A note of heartfelt thanks to the author for reminding me of many things that are so important... to laugh when it's funny, to cry when it's sad, to appreciate children for who they are, to lighten up when I should, to listen when I said I would. And most importantly, to smile just for the simple reason that my children love it when I do!"

Tarah Denesha, Domestic Engineer, Sagamore Beach, MA

"Parenting ... fishing ... It's all about being there – in the right places at the right times!"

Thomas Lanahan, Fisherman, Sagamore Beach, MA

Thanks...

...To my children, Elizabeth and Jacquelyn, for encouraging me to design my own pair of rose-tinted magnifying glasses.

...To my mother for proving that Motherhood – and Childhood – are rewarding vocations.

...To my husband, Tom, for being the father, comedian, and partner that you are!

...To my best friend, my sister, Lisa Campbell, for giving me an example by which to critique.

...To the rest of my family, for your continuous encouragement, support and hugs.

...To JoJo, Tarah, Cara, and Love, for your help with straightening socks, and so much more, these past few years.

...To everyone mentioned in this book, for being there. And to all "b-tend" persona in this book, for being an interesting part of our lives.

...To all the Mommas and Pappas who previewed my thoughts these past four years, for your eyes and ears!

...To Loretta LaRoche, for her inspirational torch, "So when's the book signing party?"

...To my favorite 'Mother and Daughter, Refine and Design Team,' Marian Atkinson and Peg Atkinson-Mavilia. Marian, for mothering me through this project; for insisting that each entry say its part. And Peg, for ensuring each page look its part! Love the awesome cover, artwork, and overall book design. Thank you so!

Momma Jeana

OXOX

Why I wrote this book

This book started as a collection of approximately a million 'post it' notes highlighting my daughters' accomplishments. They were meant to be inscribed in their baby journals but never quite made it there in the order in which they occurred.

Here's to you, girls. A unique version of your childhood journals. Some of the amusingly inspiring things you've done and said through 'our formative' years.

Unlike my mother, who became a mother at the age of twenty, I became a mother at the age of 35. It was on the day of my first baby's birth I realized Motherhood is an eternal gift. For now I have my own children to love and guide…. Yet with each hug I receive and lesson I teach, I too, acquire a world of knowledge.

My mother died nearly five years ago and in a strange way her death encouraged me to make this book a reality. Her presence in my life, and thus in my daughters' lives, is everlasting.

Here it is, Mom. The proof is in the print.

For my daughters, Elizabeth and Jacquelyn

In loving memory of my Mother, the wind beneath the wing of each and every fairy in our tales.

Contents

$\mathcal{A}$ Poem –
Enchanted Whispers:

When children speak –
They anticipate an audience

When children question –
They look for answers

When children 'pretend' –
Fact and fiction become their reality

When children look through the clouds –
They always see the sun

When children take risks –
They are on a road to discovery

When children grow –
They expand from the inside out

When children live the 'Now' of each day –
They show us the way

When children are kids –
They expect these precious moments to be savored

When children role play –
We see our own reflections in the mirror

Introduction

Like every mother of youngsters, my laundry is three days behind. Crowded countertops in my kitchen scream for organization while my children demand an audience. But I'm willing to bet that your kids are as witty and challenging, and without a doubt as captivating and convincing as mine. Therefore, I feel comfortable as a member of the Honorable Sorority of Motherhood. One who strives to breathe through the difficult moments, laugh through the funny times, and capture the monumental ones.

As far as the physical changes in me, well, I hate to admit it, but I'm definitely looking more like 'A Mother' everyday. My shoe size no longer exceeds my dress size, my hair is a tad more grey, and my attire is not quite as stylish as in years past. And yet, I am a whole lot smarter....

I'm learning that teaching children to count, unhurriedly, is not the same as coaching ourselves to count, reassuringly. (It's not the same at all.) I'm also well aware that eating my kid's leftovers, even corners of PB&J sandwiches and a few lonely tater-tots, really does count as calories. But forget about the anti-wrinkle cream which no one warned us should be applied beginning at adolescence. (Sorry Moms. It's probably a little too late!)

Yep. I'm learning it all these days. Everything that's most important anyway.

With young children to nurture and love, today is truly our most precious gift.

However, I still can't comprehend why bending and picking up a thousand toys a day doesn't count as calisthenics? Or why moving in any direction with 10 to 50 pounds in tow doesn't count as aerobics? (Mind boggling, isn't it?)

Well, enough about me already. Let me introduce our children.

It's as if I blinked and my oldest daughter, Elizabeth, celebrated her seventh birthday and boarded the big yellow school bus to first grade.
Oh, my heart.

And literally, as if I overslept one morning, Jackie, my four year old baby, was busy discovering a world of organized fun at preschool.
Oh, my soul.

There's a time when you have to explain to your children why they're born, and it's a marvelous thing if you know the reason by then.

-Hazel Scott, 1920-1981

Please don't ask me where the last seven years of my life have gone. That question could never be answered in this one little book, but parents of young children can appreciate this synopsis:

Our children have learned to eat somewhat civilly, dress themselves in clean yet unmatched clothes, recite and dial their best friend's phone numbers, and sing and dance the day through.

xiv

Suffice to say, we've been a little busy teaching each other a few worthy things. (Otherwise the kids would still be crawling around the playroom floor talking baby talk while Momma and Dadda spend their days surfing the internet.) HA!
Baby talk!? Parent time!?

The questions. The whispers. The controversies. The harmonies. The discoveries. The growth. The reality of 'it all' happened overnight, or so it seems.

When children speak –
They anticipate an audience

"When I use a word," Humpty Dumpty said in rather a scornful tone, "it means just what I choose it to mean - neither more nor less."

"The question is," said Alice, "whether you can make words mean so many different things."

"The question is," said Humpty Dumpty, "which is to be master - that's all."

Lewis Carroll (1832-1898)

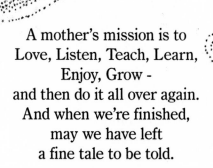

A mother's mission is to
Love, Listen, Teach, Learn,
Enjoy, Grow -
and then do it all over again.
And when we're finished,
may we have left
a fine tale to be told.

A Chatty Mom, b. 1961

When children speak...

"Mommy, me and Lizzy are just kids. You and daddy aren't kids. But know what Mommy?"

"What Jackie?"

"We can still love each other for our whole life, ya' know."

"I hope so baby!"

Life, as we know it, is an explainable course of events. Life begins in the womb and ends at death - and every day in between is a gift. The sooner we realize that life is short and precious, the better. And being promised to be loved for your whole life, WOW! What a bonus!

"And know what else Mom?"

"What, Elizabeth?"

"It's like kids can't stop talking all day."

"It sure is, Elizabeth!"

❊ ❊ ❊

Children tell it like it is, straight from their hearts. Their innocent, long-winded, wisdom-filled voices tell us exactly how and what we should be doing to live a more meaningful life. And yet, isn't their constant chatter a precious gift that reminds us to keep talking, guiding, and listening?

If a child's gift
Of communication
Is not welcomed,
Our kid's might not
Feel the need to talk at all.

2

For parents of (young) full-time receptionists...

"I'll get it," my four year-old screams as she runs toward the kitchen phone.

"Hello."...

"No. My Daddy's not home."...

"My name is Jackie."...

"Mommy's in the potty."...

"Who's this?"...

"What's your name again?"...

"Do I know you?"...

"Do you have a dog?

> *The greatest poem ever known Is one all poets have outgrown; The poetry, innate, untold, Of being only four years old.*
> *Christopher Morley (1890-1957), "To a Child"*

I have a dog named Cookie. She likes to eat cookies 'ya know."...
"What?"...
"But I don't know how to read yet."...
"I'm having grilled cheese for lunch, not steak."...
"What?"...
"We're going to Disney World next year. It's not all the way around the world, but it's really far away."...
"What?"...
"Wait a minute please. Mommy's still in the potty, but I'll bring the phone to her. What's your name again?"...
"Mommy, it's for you. It's Mick Ahomesith and he wants to take you to another world."

"Hello."...

"Hello Mrs. Lamamamm?" (Telemarketers always pronounce my name incorrectly.)

"Yes. That's me. Can I help you with something?"

"My name is Mark Yahobarosmith. I'm calling to inform you that you have qualified for a free credit rating report along with two FREE months of six of your favorite magazines. You may even be eligible for freezer full of Omaha steaks. And, just for you Mrs. Lamamamm, today only, you will be entered into our sweepstakes to win a free trip around the world! Could I just take a minute of your time to ask a few questions please?"

"Hold on a minute Sir."...

"Jackie, Mr. So-and-So wants to talk to you again."

"Hello, this is Jackie again. Can you tell me your name another time, slowly this time please?"

CLICK

"Mom! He 'hangded' up! Rats! Now we're not gonna get to go around a world!"

❊ ❊ ❊

When children don't speak, we should listen to their silence!

When my oldest daughter was about six years old, she began shying away from almost every person she did not know personally.

Today, at The Little Store (Sagamore Beach) a fellow shopper said "Hi" to my daughter and Elizabeth looked the other way. Mortified, I said, "Elizabeth, please don't be rude. That gentleman just wants to say good morning to you."

She answered a quiet "Hi", and then urged me to keep on shopping.

Later the same day, Elizabeth was busy organizing the soda chest at our former restaurant, East Wind Lobster (Buzzards Bay) when she was approached by another cheerful soul. "You look adorable dear. Are you having a special time working with your Mommy?" Elizabeth looked at the ground, and then at me, and shrugged her shoulders. No response. Nothing, despite my look of disappointment.

It was not until we had a 'heart to heart' that I realized something I should have had the sense to know already. "Elizabeth, sometimes people are just trying to be friendly. Why you don't talk to nice people when they are talking to you?"

"Because Mom, we're not supposed to talk to strangers. You told me, and Daddy told me, and we're learning all about it in school too..."

The situation improved when I delicately tried to explain that it is 'okay' to talk to (some) strangers (a little bit) when you're with someone safe.

And then came the discussion about why it's never safe to talk with most strangers.

Halfway through my lengthy explanation about 'the safety facts of life', Elizabeth said, *"I get it now. Next time I'll say 'hi' to strangers when I'm with you or Daddy, but I'll say nothing when I'm supposed to. Okay Mom?"*

"Okay Elizabeth!"

In Reflection....

As a child, I was very shy. "Reserved" my
mother used to say. But that doesn't mean
my mother didn't hear my unspoken words.
(Thanks, Mom, for listening!)

When Mommy Speaks
She definitely anticipates being heard -

"Oh Tom, why is it always my turn to clear the laundry shoot, change the sheets, wash the windows, scrub the toilets, and help the kids with their homework?

Silence...

"Tom, I just asked you a simple question."

"What?"

"Remember the story you told me about what happened to your grandmother when she turned 50? That's only seven years from now for me, Tom."

"Huh? Are you talking to me, Jean?"

"Yes! Didn't you say Nana became deaf, developed Alzheimer's and acute arthritis at an early age? And didn't Nana's doctor blame her conditions on the fact that she cleaned her house too much?"

No response.

"Tom! I'm trying to talk to you! What are you doing up there?"

"I can't hear a word you are saying, Jean. I've got the vacuum running."

"Oh! It's nothing important, Tom. I'm just reminding myself how smart some women are."

"What?"

"Nothing Tom. I just wanted to tell you that I'm making your favorite dinner. Grilled chops and cheese potatoes! But it won't be ready for twenty more minutes!"

"Great! I'll be down after I finish vacuuming the cobwebs from the ceilings!"

"No rush Dear!"

⁂ ⁂ ⁂

7

When children say 'thank you'...

Hearing young children articulate those big words tell us they are beginning to understand two very essential behaviors of life; Respect and Gratitude.

"Thank You, Mom, for making us our favorite kind of 'space ship' macaroni."

"Actually, Elizabeth, they are called 'Dischi Volenti'."

"It doesn't matter what they call them in China, 'cause we just love them." To Jackie, Elizabeth asks, "Did you say 'thank you' to Mom for making us something we like so much?"

"Thank you, Mommy. We love the macaronis too."

"Thank you, Elizabeth and Jacquelyn."

"For what, Mom?"

"For expecting me to be grateful for the little things in life."

"Huh?"

* * *

When people are nice, other people are nice to them too. Like my teachers - Miss Judy and Miss Debbie and Miss Danielle at Rainbow School. They are nice! And they teach us it's nice to say 'thank you' for our snacks and apple juice. -Jackie

(Thank you Miss Judy, Miss Debbie, and Miss Danielle! - Miss Jean)

"Hey Mom, that worker girl didn't even say
'thank you' after you gave her all of your money!
That's not very nice!"

"No, it's not very nice at all Elizabeth."

"I hope you didn't give her a tip or extra
money or anything like that Mom!"

"Not today, Baby Cakes!"

"Maybe we should find a new coffee window to go to,
Mom, where the workers are a little more friendly?"

"I think you're absolutely right, Elizabeth!"

On a very, very, light note

I knew it was time to take my children to Church when, at bedtime, my three and a half year old knelt down, folded her little arms, and into her clasped hands Jackie sang:

"God Bless America
Land at I lub…..
Stand aside her
And ride her…..
Through the night,
With a light from above."

And then she continued with her version of "A Pledge" -

"I pedge Amegience…..
to the flag
of the United States of America,

9

> *and to the Apublic*
> *for which he stands*
> *with liberty*
> *and 'ustice for all...*
> *Amen."*

"That's not right! Let me teach you again," Elizabeth says to Jackie. Upon her knees at the foot of her bed, Elizabeth bellows the correct words to *God Bless America* and *The Pledge of Allegiance*.

I let them finish before adding, "Girls, when we say our prayers, it's time to thank God for everything we are grateful for; all the people we love. And then we ask for His blessings and guidance."

"But, Mom. We just did !"

(I never did like *"Now I Lay Me Down To Sleep"*. Too many implications to explain. So I guess for now, reciting our allegiance is more appropriate.)

✳ ✳ ✳

On a very serious note

I count my blessings (everyday) and thank my husband (maybe not nearly enough) for his support in the mission of guiding our children because I definitely couldn't do this alone. NO WAY!

Thank you, Tom, for all you do and do so well! (XOXO)

When children Scream....

"Hey Mommy, guess what?"

"What Jackie?"

"Today was one of my 'bestest' days ever. ... We got to go fishing with Auntie Ellie and Uncle John and caught some little shiny fishes. Next time we will catch a really huge fish because we know how to hold the rod – like THIS. And then you twirl this 'spinny' thing LIKE THIS! ***And then you pull the rod up LIKE THIS!!!"***

Excitement is a natural high to a child. They can't control it – or hide it - for it shines through even when they're just describing a thrilling moment.

Children don't think twice about using the proper adjective to convey their gusto. Nor can they disguise a giggle, monstrous scare tactic, or squeal of delight.

And why should they? A scream is one way of expressing enthusiasm for their world – loudly and proudly!

"Mom, I just saw a sign for THE FAIR!"
Elizabeth screams from the backseat.

"I saw it too, Elizabeth. We'll be there in just a few minutes."

"I'm so excited too, Mommy! I'm getting goose 'bumpies' all over myself!!!" Jackie yells.

"Cool. Let me see them, Jackie!" Elizabeth sings in her
very loud, very soprano voice.

❄ ❄ ❄

What about when Mommy screams?

She's either extremely excited or utterly insistent upon being heard. (Or maybe, she's just plain scared?)

"Mommy, you didn't have to yell so loud two times! I heard you the first time."

"Then why didn't you come when I asked you to, Jackie?"

"Because I just wanted to hear how loud you could yell my name, my whole name, JACQUELYN R.... L.........!!!!!"

* * *

When it comes to your children, what are you afraid of most?

I asked a few mothers this loaded question and was amazed at the similar responses – and the quality of their screams!

Besides the trivial stuff, like constantly arriving late to every invited event, all mothers expressed utmost worry for the safety of our children. Our world.

"It's difficult enough to explain the actions of villains in my kids' fairy tales. Now we are forced to explain acts of terrorism – for real!"

And all mothers were highly concerned about her efforts in guiding her children to make the *right* choices in the *wrong* situations. When compiled, the results sounded like this:

"I hope to be teaching my child to
stand firm when she knows the right answer;
stand tall when she argues for the crowd;
stand straight when taking responsibility for her actions;
and run away from the gang when they are
headed along the wrong path."

In addition, every mother had very loud words to convey that her children don't appreciate that she, too, was a daughter not so long ago. (Here's where the screaming starts.) And then came the realization that her young children, of her own flesh and blood, would someday (way too soon), grow into adolescence. Yikes!

So Moms, besides the safety of our children, what are we afraid of most?

<u>Growth? Stagnation?</u> **<u>Teenagers (like ourselves)??!!!</u>**

Our young children will grow up. In the meantime, let's Pray, practice what we know, and learn what we don't because (here's the terrifying part)....

"YOU MAY BECOME A GRANDPARENT SOME DAY!"

Oh my! My Mother boldly said those same words not so long ago! Only she spelled it 'REVENGE'!

❊ ❊ ❊

When children shout, "It's very important" ...

Notice any differences here?

"Mommy, help!"
"What is it, Jackie?"
"I need some help putting on my socks so the lumpy parts are all gone."

"Where are you Mom?"
"I'm right here, Elizabeth."
"Oh. I just wanted to make sure you didn't go outside to play in the garden without us."

"Momma, I really need to tell you something important!"

"Go ahead, Jackie. I'm listening."

"Mommy, I know the "f" word is a bad word."

Did she just say what I thought she said?

"Mommy, didn't you hear me? I said, I know that the 'f' word is a bad word."

I can't ignore her statement again. I'm petrified, yet somewhat curious to hear what's next. I refrain from yelling, WHO TAUGHT YOU THAT? Instead, cautiously I sigh, "Which bad word are you talking about, Jackie?"

"I can't say it Mom, 'cause you'll send me to my room. I was just telling you that I know the "f" word is a bad word."

"Well, Jackie, why don't you just tell me the "f" word and then we can discuss it."

"You won't get mad at me, Mom?"

"No, because I asked you to tell me. So what is it, Baby?"

"Okay Mom, sound it out." Jackie's showing her teeth and puckering her lips as she instructs, "do this with your mouth and say SH...SH...SH....in your teeth."

I follow the orders and say "sh.. sh... sh..." through my teeth.

"Do you know what it is now, Mom?"

"No, not really. 'SH' what, Jackie?"

*"Mommy, the "f"word is **SHUT UP!** And that's a really bad word."*

"MOOOMMM! THIS IS VERY IMPORTANT!!!"

"Elizabeth, I'm right here. What is it?"

"Quick Mom! Look out this window. There's a baby bird peeking out of his nest. You have to sit quietly and watch. His daddy is gonna teach him to fly right now!"

(Is it my imagination or are there more birds, squirrels, and butterflies – than ever before - living in our backyards?)

$\mathcal{A}$t-ten-tion Parents!

Here are some questions we must consider regarding
our V.I.P. mission:

How Do We

* Nurture our children's enthusiasm for nature, the beauty around
us - If we don't take the time to watch a bird make its maiden
flight?

* Teach our children about sensitivity and compassion - If we
pretend to be made of steel?

* Encourage our children to strive for their goals – If we settle for
less than we deserve? Or desire?

* Teach our babies to read - If we don't read with them?

* Encourage our kids to think "out of the box" – If our thoughts
are linear? Predictable? Boring?

* Prove to our children the value of true friendship – If we don't
reach out and touch those we care about? Or those in need?

* Explain to our kids the worth of a "value meal" – If they haven't
had to count nickels to buy one (for herself and her best friend)?

* Show our children the strength of a smile - If we spend much of
our time wearing an upside down smile?

* Explain the depth of a whisper – If we're too preoccupied to
listen closely?

When children whisper...

"Mom, I just want to tell Jackie one little secret before she goes to her first day of preschool." Loud enough for me to hear, Elizabeth whispers, *"Jackie, don't be afraid of your new school. There will be kids that you don't know, but when I get home you can tell me all about your new friends and about the cool stuff you did. I have to go now 'cause it's my first day at first grade. I LOVE YOU Jackie."*

"I LOVE YOU TOO," Jackie's Irish whisper sings into her sister's ear.

At Preschool.......

"Mommy, before you leave me at my new school, I just have to tell you a secret."

"Jackie, I have to get to work, so can you tell me your secret now?"

Into my ear she breathes, *"I love you a million bucks. And Mom, when it's time to pick me up, please take the shortcut so you won't be the last Mom to pick up her kid. Okay Mommy?"*

"I'll be the first one here today. And Jackie, I love you four million bucks," I whisper into her smiling ear.

Later the same day...

L - Jackie, Who did you play with at preschool today?
J - Jake.
L - Jackie, do you lllllluuuuuuuvvvvvvv Jake?
J - Yes.
L - Jackie, are you gonna mmaaaaarrrrrryyyyy Jake?
J - His name is not Mary! IT'S JAKE!!
L - I said Jake. I asked if you are gonna marry Jake?
J -NO! Girls can't marry boys who are their friends!

When I questioned Jackie about the "not marrying a friend" part, she clarified it to mean, *Me and Jake are just friends, not wedding friends. Besides, Mom, I can't get married 'till I have a baby!*"

OH BOY! I'll question her more about that one in a few years......

❆ ❆ ❆

$\mathcal{A}$bout listening -
The skilled art of hearing, really hearing, which our children do so naturally!

My daughters were watching the 'Wiggles' show on the Disney channel this morning. As all mothers of youngsters know, the Wiggles speak with a strong Australian accent and they love to create in the kitchen.

"*Hey Mom, we should try this new recipe. The Wiggles are making a pizza that has 'saaawwwdeens' on it.*"

"The pizza has 'what' on it, Elizabeth?"

"*You know, Mom. Those little fish called 'saaawwwdeens'.*"

"I think they are called 'sardines', Elizabeth."

"*No, they are called 'saaawwwdeens'! That's what the Wiggles' chef called them.*"

"That's because they live in Australia and speak with an accent different than ours."

"*Show me on the map Mom. ...Well, no matter where he lives, he thinks they're called 'saaawwwdeeens' so that's what I want to call them too!*"

When parents are enthusiastic spectators... We hear (and see) everything. Every little thing!

We amaze our children when we say "I heard that" while engaged in a serious conversation on the telephone. And when we hear a big thump from the next room, we instinctively shout, "Ouch! Are you alright?"

But what about when you're watching your child as she attempts to steal another piece of candy from the forbidden candy jar? She sees your eyes, piercing directly into hers, so how can we possibly monitor her every move at the same time?

"I told you. Mommy knows everything!"

"WOW. That's awesome Mommy!"

So here we are, another generation of mothers who can hear and see our children (and husbands) while making a *Mr. Clean Magic Eraser* crumble. We can do *that* while reciting a spelling bee and making two different kinds of sandwiches. And we can do *that* while sorting laundry and chatting with a mortgage expert about refinancing our homes.

Of course we can do all that! (We've been trained very well.)

* * *

"Tom, can you hear me now?"

"Loud and clear, Buttercup!"

"Just checking, Dumpling!"

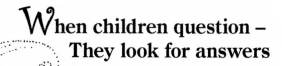

**When children question –
They look for answers**

*The important thing is not
to stop questioning. Curiosity has its
own reason for existing.*
Albert Einstein (1879-1955)

QUESTIONS:

Q is for Query
U is for Unveiling
E is for Enrichment
S is for Sincerity
T is for Tenacity
I is for Instinct
O is for Opportunity
N is for Never-ending
S is for Satisfaction!

When children Question...

Children ask 'Who, How, Why, What, When, Where, How Come, and Right Mommy?' so frequently because they need and want to know more. Sometimes they want to know about something totally mystifying - like the exact workings of a jet plane engine. *"How does a plane fly through the air? And how can it land on such a tiny piece of land?"*

And sometimes, children just need to be reassured of the fact that they are the most vital beings in our world.
"Mommy, Daddy, where are you? Did you finish making my favorite breakfast yet?"

But more often than that, children are plain nosey, and want to know about everything and anything now!
"Who are you talking to on the phone, Mom? Are you talking to Tarah and planning a play date? Just shake your head 'yes' or 'no'! Please. I have to know!"

* * *

How does a parent deal with answering approximately sixty questions per hour, per waking child? Here's a few suggestions:

Yes, that's so unfair, but so true…..

Ah huh! The world is a funny place….

Maybe another day, Sweetie….

You are absolutely right, but not right now…

I know, I know. We'll have to work on that one….

Or you could use my mother's favorite: "Because I'm the Mom AND I SAID SO!"

For Fun:

Once we have abused the right to use and reuse responses from the previous list, (in my estimation by 10:30 am), try this. Answer your child's questions as if you're taking a post graduate program entrance exam.

Momma, why do birds have wings?

"Birds were given wings so they can reach appropriate altitudes to arrive at their desired destinations in adequate time. (That's why.)"

How come dogs have to go to the bathroom outside, Mommy?

"Dogs relieve themselves outdoors because they have four legs and no arms. Four legs atop a public toilet in which the aforementioned animal cannot reach – or hold - the toilet paper is totally against the law. (And that's the end of the story.)"

Were all Moms born to be the boss?

"Actually, Moms were born to rule the world. But besides that, we are completely in charge of our children until they can earn a living of six or more figures, at which point, children will be granted the opportunity to adopt their mothers. (Don't worry; I'll explain it all to you again in a few years.)"

Those answers should keep your little ones thinking for a few minutes.

(And if the kids are quiet, let them be. Just be sure not to step on any cracks during the silence. We can never have too much luck you know!)

Wʰen I was a baby.......

*"Hey Mom, **when I was a baby,** did I walk like this?"*

"Well, first you crawled, and then you walked 'like that', Jackie."

*"Mom, **when I was a baby,** did I drink milk from your boobies or a bubba?"*

"Actually, from both Jackie."

*"Cool. Hey Mom, **when I was a baby,** like two years old, did I know how to color?"*

"Not very well, but you did try."

*"**When I was a baby,** you know, just born, did you hold me like this, Mommy?"*

"Very much so, Jackie. Just hold your baby close and she'll feel loved."

*"And Mom, **when I was a baby,** did I know how to talk or did I say 'DaDa' for Daddy?"*

"Why don't you go and ask Daddy that question, and whatever other questions you come up with? Okay, Jackie?"

*"That's a good idea Mommy. ... Hey Daddy, **when I was a baby.........??????"***

❊ ❊ ❊

ℙarents have many questions too

I don't want to call it paranoia, but at some point in all of our young children's lives doesn't every parent speculate that our children are, how do I say it kindly, "unique"?

I join the group, particularly after witnessing my four year old walk around the room, point her finger at people and things, and chant the words 'Abee, Abee'."

We must have a mother/daughter chat.....

"Jackie, why do you walk around pointing and chanting 'Abee, Abee' so many times a day?"

"Mommy, I'm not saying 'Abee'. I'm saying 'A BEE'! Like I'm a scary bumble bee who's gonna sting somebody with my big stinger finger. Remember that day when Lizzy got stung by three bees? She ran around saying 'A BEE' all week long."

And the same mother has other questions when overhearing my seven year old say that she did not finish her assignment because she "couldn't wait to use the computer".

"Elizabeth, why were you more concerned about the computer than your studies at school today?"

"Because Mom, my assignment was on the computer and we ran out of time. But don't worry. My teacher told me I'm first to use the computer tomorrow. You'll be very proud when you see what I can do on the computer at school, Mom."

It's settled. My children are normal. (It's only their mother I question!) Ha!

In order to successfully meet the challenges of parenting, we need to humbly admit:

We don't know everything. We'll never have all the right solutions! And yet, we must continue to search for answers. (What other choice do we have anyway?)

※ ※ ※

When children Wonder........

Elizabeth: *Mom, I wonder if I'm going to lose all my teeth before the big ones grow in. Look at all the teeth I'm missing! The tooth fairy must have lots of teeth in Fairyland.*

Mom: Elizabeth, I'm sure your smile will be filled with big sparkling teeth soon. And yes, the tooth fairy must have oodles of teeth by now!

Jackie: *What does the tooth fairy do with our teeth, Mommy? Are they like treasures in Fairyland or something? And what is a fairy anyway? Is she magical or is she pretend?*

When the first baby laughed for the first time, the laugh pieces broke into a thousand pieces and they all went skipping about, and that was the beginning of fairies. And now when every baby is born its first laugh becomes a fairy. So there ought to be one fairy for every boy or girl.

J.M. Barrie (1860-1937)

24

Mom: Little teeth are definitely treasures in Fairyland, Jackie. And fairies, they are about as magical and enchanting as you want them to be. Now about your teeth. Girls, did you brush them? All of them?

So this is what my mother implied when she said, "Wait till you're a mother. You'll know what it all means then. And the tooth fairy, you'll learn about her powers too... Just wait!"

In My Pre-Children Days:

❋ The tooth fairy had a sachet full of nickels and pennies
❋ My lipstick had a cover, and my blush, an applicator
❋ I had a first name
❋ At mealtime, my dog got fed a bowl full of 'Kibbles and Bits'
❋ I yelled (only) when I was angry
❋ My husband and I went into the same bed at the same time
❋ I thought my mother's rules were cruel
❋ I drove myself to my play dates
❋ I got dressed to go to work
❋ Children belonged to someone else
❋ I knew not of the power of wonder!

The Power of Wonder

In the shower this morning, I was wondering if my body has the ability to defy aging – mainly, its affects. Some things get finer with age. Right? So why can't my buttocks and thighs? Anyway, the 'wondering session' gets real weird.

I wondered about June Cleaver and what she may be doing with her time these days. Certainly her kids are grown and gone from home. Ward has to be retired; June must have a driver's license by now.

And then came the visions of how she spends her days. ... June wakes at 6:10 and serves fresh fruit and brewed coffee at her linen covered table. She's dressed in a stylish leotard under her neatly ironed warm-up suit. (And, yes, June still sports small pearl earrings.)

Off she goes for a 22 minute walk around the neighborhood. After drinking freshly squeezed juice to wash down a mega pack of vitamins, June safely leads her 700 series BMW to the 7:45 yoga class where nine perfectly manicured white and silver/blue haired women stretch and meditate for one hour. Next stop, the library, to discuss this week's book club reading assignment: *Man's Search for Meaning (by Viktor Frankel)*.

After reflecting upon the miracles of living, June hurries to her son's house before Beaver's red headed twins descend from high school bus. June continues to do what she's done all her life – she mothers everyone and everything around her. Then she hurries home, allowing plenty of time to prepare Ward's dinner - a 400 calorie, low fat, low cholesterol, protein enriched, high in fiber, home-cooked masterpiece.

After the china is hand washed and put away, June changes into an *Armani* pant suit and *Manolo Blahnik* shoes and off she goes! At exactly 6:28 pm, Mrs. Cleaver's gavel marks 'A Call To Order' at the 6:30 pm RNC proceedings.

Please tell me that I'm not the only mother to wonder about what others mothers have done/didn't do/will do/want to do with her time (and kids/body/career)!!

* * *

When children ask for assistance...

*Mommy, you can close the door because I can go potty all by myself now. I need some 'privally' anyway. I'll call you when I'm done.....
Okay, I'm done! And Mommy, I think I need a little help in here.*
- Jackie

Children will always need our support, even when they wear "big girl" pants.

'Borrowed' Fingers

I learned some very interesting facts today: *Tomatoes can dance, lettuce has wings, bacon sings, and friends can borrow their friend's fingers.*

The school bus dropped Elizabeth off at 3:15 pm and the phone rang almost immediately. *"Mom, it's for me. It's going to be Montana 'cause I invited her over for dinner. She likes whatever you cook, so please, just say 'yes' Mom?"*

No one of us knows more than all of us together!
Marian & Maureen

"Elizabeth, we have to check with her mother first. It's fine with me, but Stephanie may have other plans. Understand?!"

"Yep", Elizabeth yells before she screams, *"Hi Montana"* into the telephone.

Stephanie had no plans so she brings Montana over and surprises my four year old with an invitation to go and play with Shanny, Montana's younger sister. (I guess you would call it an impromptu kid swapping extravaganza.)

27

Tonight's dinner party consisted of me and two first graders sitting in front of the makings of BLT sandwiches. My maternal senses told me that the girls were not at all interested in answering my invasive questions about their day at school. So I ate my sandwich quickly, but cleaned the kitchen slowly.

All the while I watched as ordinary pieces of food grew into a new life form. Sliced tomatoes became dancing fairies, lettuce grew wings, and strips of bacon sang like rock stars.

I enjoyed the silliness until the girls reached a point where they could laugh no more. (Oh, how I remembered that weakness. That senseless, awesome feeling!)

"Okay girls. Wash your hands and get ready to do your math homework."

The girls sat side by side with a piece of paper and a deck of math cards. *"Liz, the next card asks us to add 8 plus 4. We don't have enough fingers to count that high,"* Montana admitted. Bewildered, the girls look at each other, until they figured out a plan. *"Here Montana, you can borrow four of my fingers, if that's how many you need,"* Elizabeth offered.

Together their bouncing chins touched each of Montana's eight fingers and then four more of Liz's 'borrowed' fingers.

"Mom/Jean, we got the answer to this problem. It's 12."

"Good job, girls."

They flip another card. *"This card asks us to add 9 plus 14. No way do we have enough fingers to do that!"* I heard the girls admit.

I watched them count their fingers one at a time and then one at a time again. It takes a few minutes before they ask,

"Mom/Jean, can we borrow some of your fingers please?"

✳ ✳ ✳

"Never doubt that a small group of thoughtful,
committed citizens can change the world.
Indeed, it's the only thing that ever has."
Margaret Mead (1901-1978)

When children seek Justice...

Even though parents think they can fight their children's battles and protect them from every disappointment – WE CAN'T!

But giving our children the knowledge that they are loved, no matter what, is a good beginning.

"Mom, sometimes I ask one of my friends if I can sit with them on the school bus and they say 'No'. May I please bring some Barbies in my backpack tomorrow? At least then it won't be like I'm sitting all alone!"

"Sure you can, Elizabeth. But first come and give me a big hug! ... I wish I was on your bus so that I could sit with you everyday."

"But Mom, mothers aren't allowed on the school bus, unless we're going on a field trip or something."

"Well, sign me up for the next field trip please."

"Awesome! Thanks Mom!"

* * *

Life is not always fair. It's sometimes downright cruel and can bring out the best - or the worst - in us. The way we deal with life's disappointments makes us who we are. However, the simple truth is this:

If our self esteem
depends on the approval of others,
we're destined to be
easily disappointed or hurt....

29

How to get (a little bit of) justice for your children:

It's probably a good thing that Mothers are not allowed on the yellow school bus. (Besides, we'd be kicked off rather quickly after we squeezed the cheeks and squished the snacks of the bullies on the bus.) We'd surely have some explaining to do if we were allowed to do or say the first things that come to mind when confronting the kids responsible for teasing or harassing more innocent children.

But relax Moms.

Are WE not responsible for organizing the social affairs of our children?

Aren't WE the ones who coordinate the gala event with parents of 'the good kids' on the school bus?

Don't WE send out the invitations?

Isn't it OUR JOB to stuff the goody bags?

* * *

"Mommy, something is not fair around here."

"Like what, Jackie?"

"How come you let me buy chocolate ice cream at the grocery store but you never let us eat it after supper?"

"That's because, Jackie, we don't eat chocolate when it's close to bedtime."

"Then can I have some for breakfast? That would be fair Mom, because breakfast is not at nighttime."

"We'll see."

"Cool! Hey Elizabeth. Mom just said we could have chocolate ice cream for breakfast tomorrow!"

* * *

ℋbout 'Fairness, Equal Opportunity' at our house

By the time my youngest celebrated her third birthday, I had already sung approximately 11,000 lullabies. And based on the same simple calculation, I had definitely read, or made up, at least 4,000 good night stories.

"Okay girls, it's time to go to the bathroom before we go upstairs and read a story. Say good-night to Daddy," I add with some firmness.

"Good-night Daddy," Jackie hums.

"Good-night Dad. I...love.....you.....," my oldest says, stalling, thinking of a monumental way to avoid going to bed this minute.

"Wait a minute. Mom, there's a little problem here," Elizabeth adds with a perplexed look about her. *"Why do you always get to read to us and sing songs and tuck us in every night? Daddy never gets to do all that. Why doesn't Daddy ever get a turn, Mom?"*

I had no idea where this conversation was going, but decided to play with it a little.

"Elizabeth, you are so smart to think about fairness. Poor Daddy doesn't get to do anything fun at nighttime except watch TV all by himself. I feel so bad. How could we have overlooked this for so long?"

"You have to let Daddy have a turn. That's only fair, Mom."

I'm having real fun now! "Lizzy, you are so right. Of course it's Dad's turn to tuck you in tonight, because it was my turn last night, and the night before, and the night before. Poor Daddy. He deserves a whole lot more, don't you think?"

"Yes, Mom. We 'gotta' get more fair! That means it's Daddy's turn to take us to bed now, and your turn the next night, and Daddy after that. Sorry Mom," Elizabeth adds with equality in her tone.

"It's okay, Lizzy. I completely understand. Life is not always fair - but in this household, we sure do try!"

"But Mom, you know I have homework to do when you bring the girls to bed," Daddy says, adding to the drama.

Elizabeth is now very concerned. *"Daddy, you don't go to college, Mommy does, so she's the one with the homework. C'mon Daddy, we gotta go read our story book now!"*

✳ ✳ ✳

What a beautiful sight. Three of my favorite people are standing on the landing reciting together:

"Goodnight Mom. I love you."

"Goodnight Momma. Don't let the bed bugs bite."

"Goodnight Honey. Thank you for teaching us about fairness."

"Yes, Virginia, there is a Santa Claus"

("It's a Wonderful Life" 1946)

…And he's sound asleep in my girls' room right now.

✳ ✳ ✳

When children disobey...

Mommy, I didn't mean to hit Lizzy, but she took my markers and crumpled up my papers. Then she stuck her tongue out at me. Do I have to sit on the time-out chair for a long time, even if I already said 'Sorry'? - Jackie

"Mommy, Lizzy's bossin me."	"Mommy, Jackie's feet are touching me."
"Am not."	*"Are not."*
"Am too."	*"Are too."*
"Am not."	*"Are not."*
"Am too!"	*"Are too!"*

Excuse me for one minute! My children are expressing themselves in an unacceptable manner while they decide what's right, what's theirs, perhaps both, or perhaps neither. Now I have to figure out who won last time, or something equally as difficult!

This topic deserves a book of its own, but here's an abridgment:

Disciplining, which is about as much fun as a being assigned a 'time out', requires patience, big ears, and big feet to hold ground when you're sinking deeper and deeper into the manure. But stand tall, because disciplining, the core of parenting, is all about teaching absolute truth - from head to feet.

Teaching total and complete truth that will last for all time is not an easy task, especially when parents are so busy clarifying one moment at a time.

It means - continually striving for absolute truth.

It means – confidently walking on solid ground.

It means - our children are counting on us to show them the way.

* * *

It's difficult to find yourself
"locked-in" by a judgment
made in haste.
But if the rules are clear,
and fair, you're stuck with it.
Forever!
(So think before you speak!)

* * *

My daughters' definitions of 'Time Out':

When we're bad, we have to sit on the black chair in the corner for a long time and think about it. – Elizabeth

And that's not fun because other kids get to play while I'm by myself, all alone, thinking and thinking about naughty stuff. – Jackie

My explanation of 'Time Out':

A moment of quiet time (supposedly) for Mom to figure out the response to her child's last move.

My mother's description of 'Time Out':

I once asked my mother why she never used the 'Time Out Method' as a disciplinary tool when we were growing up. Her reply was something like this:

"It's ridiculous that we tell young children to sit quietly and think about what they did wrong. They know what they did and need discipline when the wrong doing occurred. Not ten minutes later!"

(Boy, that makes a whole lot of sense now!)

❋ ❋ ❋

How can our children change their moods so quickly? And when they do, how can a mere temperament change alter every one of their precious little features?

When my children are "good" they're pure, so beautiful. As if meticulously chiseled from fine porcelain.

When my children are "bad" they're tainted, down right ugly. Like a sculpture spat together with crusty play dough!

When children 'pretend' –
Fact and fiction become their reality

* * *

*One of the virtues of being very young
is that you don't let facts get in the way
of your imagination.*
Sam Levenson

(1911-1980)

* * *

"Hey Mommy, did you say 'ready or not here I come' yet?"
"No, Jackie. I'm still counting."
*"Say it when your done and then come and try to find me. Just
don't look behind the couch for a girl dressed like a real princess.
Okay Mommy?"*
"Okay Jackie. Ready or not, here I come!"

When children 'pretend' ...

"Jackie, let's pretend it's our birthday today."

"Okay, Lizzy. Let me get some towels so we can wrap up stuff we already have in our toy box."

"We need three towels please, Jackie."

"Lizzy, do you want games or dollies for your 'b-tend' birthday?"

"Surprise me! And then we'll surprise Mom with a birthday present too."

As I unwrap a kitchen towel holding a naked Barbie Doll with ink scribbling on her face, I ask myself, "Why is it so easy to lose unself-conscious wonder as we grow older?"

* * *

We went to a play yard place with Auntie Susan and Mike and I got to climb a rock building! For real, Mom! I put my foot inside the rock and climbed right up the building. Just like a real spider lady.
– Elizabeth

And Mommy, I climbed up the rock building like a super hero person. Just like a real Power Puff Girl. -Jackie

Aren't children geniuses? Every game is filled with fresh ideas, ready to assume a new dimension in a moment's notice. Not only do kids have a gift of keeping life unpredictable, they are inspirational too!

Participating in a child's world of pretend brings us closer into their minds, spirits, and lives. March with children to the 'when fantasy becomes reality' beat of their drums. Observe and become! Perhaps it's just what the doctor ordered for reducing stress in our busy adult lives.

Advice given to anxiety ridden adults sounds something like this:

"Listen to these (twenty) 60 minute tapes, attend at least 15 yoga sessions, and keep a journal. Relax. Meditate as often as you can. Let's meet again next Thursday to evaluate your progress. Go, enjoy life. ... (Good luck.)"

A child achieves knowledge through adventure.
And yet, during their precious journey they need to be guided, loved, comforted, and rewarded every step of their way.

Wait a minute!
Aren't adults in search of magical experiences too?

My children are reminding me that we are.

What the expert should have said is this:

"Live a little. Laugh a lot. Go 'play' with your children! They deserve it and you need it! Call me in a month or two so we can chat about your progress. ... (Have fun!)"

❄ ❄ ❄

When children dance and sing....

Can we turn on our 'Kids Bop' tape and have a dance party, Mom? I can dance real good now! Watch me do my tapdance.
— Elizabeth

Dance parties are one of our favorite pastimes, although truthfully, none of us are very good at it. I look quite awkward, especially considering today's dance standards. (No matter how hard I try, I cannot groove to the beat.)

The littlest girl in our dance group resembles a skipping monkey, or a spinning top. Sometimes both. So, all of her moves are matchless. And my older dance partner, the 'Choreographer' she calls herself, encourages us to add drama and flamboyance to our moves. Quite frankly, her routines are remarkable. Similar to those of Elaine on the 'Seinfeld' show.

(Be sure to catch Elaine boogie on 'Seinfeld' reruns. Elaine may not dance like Gretta Garbo, but she sure knows how to have a good time!)

* * *

And then there are the singing parties. Lots of singing parties at our house!

Teach a child a song
and she'll sing it to her world.

"Momma's Gonna Teach You How to Fly"
(a song to my girls)

Hush little baby don't you cry;
Momma's gonna teach you how to fly.
Over the mountains through the sky;
Over the tree tops oh so high.
Hush little baby don't you cry;
Momma's gonna be there to dry your eye.
Hush little baby don't you cry;
Momma's gonna teach you how to fly!

Come here, Auntie Be. I gotta dry your eye.... Want to sing 'Mommy's Flying' song again? This time we should dress up when we sing. You can be Auntie, or a Grandmother, or a Princess, or a Fairy Godmother, or whoever you want. Let me get some make-up and hats! – Jackie

*A child loves to play,
not because it's easy, but
because it's hard.
Benjamin Spock
(1903-1998)*

When children fly...

"Want to try something cool, Mom?"
"Sure."
"Stand on the couch, next to me. Hook this towel into the collar of your shirt. Now, close your eyes and jump in the air and make a wish. Do this (spread your arms) when you jump and then keep them out till your feet hit the rug. Watch us fly first..."
"Oh boy! You girls want me to jump that high?"
"Mom, you can do it. All it takes is a little bit of fairy dust. Let me sprinkle you with some pretend dust."
"Ready, set, here I go!"
"Wow! You know how to fly too, Mom!"

Soon you'll zoom all around the room
All it takes is faith and trust
But the thing that's a positive must
Is a little bit of pixie dust
The dust is a positive must

You can fly! You can fly!
You can fly! You can fly!

Music: Sammy Fain; Lyrics: Sammy Cahn; Coaches: Elizabeth and Jacquelyn

To the Moon and Back

After learning to fly in the playroom today, I was blessed with the opportunity to go outside and search for a new species of birds, study beautiful weeds, and build our own version of a worm farm. Then we took a ride in a wagon, which transformed into a fishing vessel. We enjoyed snacks at a picnic table, until it converted into a deserted tropical island surrounded by hungry sharks and playful dolphins. We rested on a hammock – for about two minutes – while we encouraged the ropes to grow wings that flew us straight to the moon!

All upon a wishes' command!

※ ※ ※

One can never consent to creep when one feels an impulse to soar. - Helen Keller (1880-1968)

$\mathcal{B}$ut Sometimes, Mom needs to fly solo!

When we have the urge to go shopping when it's not even "Completely Out of Groceries Day," it's because we need to spread our independent wings (and sing all of our favorite songs) ALONE!

But mothers are never alone - even when we are by ourselves.

As I'm wedged in a line of cars at the nearest drive-through Latte' shop, I hear the voices:

Mommy, where's my Lilo and Stitch video?

Mommy, where's my new 'learn to tell time' watch that Lou and Barbara gave me for Christmas?

Honey, where's my other boot?

"Where you all left them. That's where!" I shout as I turn up the volume to a good Jimmy Buffet tune and opt to take the long route to the mall. (We can do without Yoplait and Keeblers for one night. Momma needs a new bra!)

Wⁿhen children smile and act silly...

"Did you see Auntie Marnie's teeth shine? I think it's because she smiles so big. I want my teeth to be shiny too, so I'm gonna smile bigger. ... How do my teeth look now Mom?"

"They look sparkling, healthy, and happy, Elizabeth. Just like the rest of you."

In addition to the weather conditions, which may or may not affect their play time at the park, most children recognize the difference between ordinarily miserable or exceptionally miserable people. And they immediately identify the elite, those remarkably cheerful persons whom we may get a glimpse of occasionally.

Smile Mommy... Happy people have big faces - and now you have a 'gigantrick' face too! - Jackie

It's been proven:
The more you smile,
the bigger your face
will grow,
the brighter your teeth
will appear,
and the happier
you will feel!

Here's another bit of sweet truth:
The more you smile,
the more your
children will too!
(I kid you not!)

"Let's do a joke, Mommy."
"Okay. You can start, Jackie."
"Why did the boy throw butter out the window?"
"I don't know. Why did the boy throw butter out the window?"
"Because he wanted to see a piece of butter fly, like a butterfly!"
"Oh, that's so funny, Jackie."

"Mom, do you want to hear a song I just made up?"
"Sure, Elizabeth. Go ahead."
"It's called K I S S I and G."
(big breath)
"Mommy and Daddy 'sittin' in the tree -
K I S S I and G.
First comes LUV
Then comes marrying;
Then comes Mommy
in a baby carriage!... Isn't that so funny, Mom? Mommy and
Daddy marrying and then getting a mommy in a baby carriage."
"That is hilarious, Elizabeth. Very funny!!"

❄ ❄ ❄

"Girls, I have to go to work now. See you in a little while!
I love you!" I yell as I skip down the walkway (the silly way
that Auntie Kim taught us).

"Bye Mom. Love
you too! Don't forget
to wear my wig and
hat at work today,"
Elizabeth yells.

"And don't forget to
tell your customers the
'knocker' joke I taught
you," Jackie screams
into the road.

Today, when I put
on a paper wig and
floppy hat, I drove
through a crowded
Sagamore Bridge
Rotary and smiled
at the New York
drivers.

An Observation Game

Next time you go out to lunch or dinner at a busy hotspot, look around. Can you spot one person holding a clipboard, cell phone, checkbook, and dirty napkins she found on the floor?
Look closely.
Is she wearing her daughter's butterfly clips in her untamed hair? Can you see a faint peanut butter and jelly handprint on her shoulder?
Now look into her eyes. Closer please.
Does she have a vested interest in the chaos or what?
"Can I help the next person please?"

Speaking of Working Moms....

We all work, hard and long.
Now comes a little fantasy to play with:
Wouldn't it be great if we went (out of the house)
to work, let's say during the 'bewitching hours',
but got compensated for our full day's efforts. ...
That is assuming there's someone responsible
for "mothering" our world during our escape.
Someone with as much energy as our children
and as much determination as ourselves.
Someone who loves to sing songs,
play hide-and-go-seek, match odd socks,
and clip little kids' toe nails.
Ha! Ha!

Wʰen children look through the clouds – They always see the sun

* * *

*A pessimist sees only the
dark side of the clouds, and mopes;
a philosopher sees both sides, and shrugs;
an optimist doesn't see the clouds at all -
he's walking on them.*
Leonard Louis Levinson
www.brainyquotes.com

*Sunshine, clouds,
or rain,
Be it hot or cold -
Follow your children;
See the joy unfold!*

-Momma Jeana

45

When children look through the clouds...

Sunny days offer the chance to explore rocks or collect sea creatures at the beach. Rainy days are an invitation to jump in puddles or search for worms and pretty rainbows. And cloudy days, they unite the senses – sort of!

Mommy, look! I see some blue spots in the sky. And I can see the baby apples growing on that tree. But we'd better hurry to go outside and play, Mommy, before the sun gets pushed back into the sky by the rain! – Jackie

"What apple tree?" I ask myself while searching for the box of sidewalk chalk. Oh, she must be referring to the little peach tree in the back yard....Wow! Can she actually see that far?

❋ ❋ ❋

Rats! It's raining! But that's okay because now my tomato plants make big tomatoes and my sunflowers will grow yummy seeds. Let's get our raincoats and check it out! –Elizabeth

❋ ❋ ❋

Unlike adults who have a way of lamenting over yesterday's hardships and anticipating tomorrow's potential disasters, children remind us that ordinary (even frustrating) occurrences can be transformed into something extraordinary and memorable. Easily!

So instead of griping about the weather, why not do what the kids do and go with the flow?

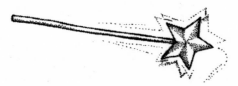

*On a drizzly Spring morning, We can put
on rubber gloves and polish silver for next
Thanksgiving's dinner or we can put on
gardening gloves and plant daffodils with our
children.*

*(For fun - Ask a grandmother what she'd do today given the
chance to do things differently.)*

When children see our flaws...

*"Good morning, Mommy. It's time to get up because it's 'sixteen
forty o'clock'. See the sun?"*

"Jackie, I'm up. And yes, I see the sun quite clearly," I say
through a yawn.

*"Mommy, do that again. Now keep your mouth open. ... What's
all those black and gold things on your big teeth? And why does your
tongue look so big and yucky?" Jackie, who is close enough to be
breathing my breaths, asks.*

*She persists at inspecting every inch of my face and continues
with the questions. "What are those marks on your forehead and
these liney things near your eyes? And what's this 'dit' thing on your
chin?"*

"Jackie, it's just my face! Those lines and 'dit' things are there
to tell the world that I'm getting older. That's all!"

*"Well, I'm getting older too, Mom. But it's time to get up and
make some pancakes 'cause I'm real hungry for pancakes."*

* * *

When children reassure us that despite our imperfections we are still lovable, that's called "unconditional love". When children realize that no matter how hard we strive for perfection, we will still make mistakes, that's called "absolute humanity".

❄ ❄ ❄

"Mom! Today was 'show and tell' day at school and I didn't have anything in my backpack to tell about because you cleaned everything out and left my bunny pictures on the table!"

"Oh, I'm sorry, Elizabeth. I forgot that today was 'show and tell'."

"I know you didn't mean to leave them out, but I really want to tell everyone about my new bunny. Can you please put a note in my bag to ask the teacher if I can do 'show day' tomorrow?"

"Let's sit down and write it together, Elizabeth."

❄ ❄ ❄

ℰpeaking of mistakes...

I have thrown away coloring books with 18 yet to be colored pages and I've vacuumed up more *Polly Pocket* accessories than I can count.

I have sent my kids to school - clad in red, white and blue the day before "red, white, and blue day", and I've forgotten to pack snacks on their designated snack day.

I have yelled at people who only deserved a reprimand, and once, regrettably, I fired an employee because she was demonstrating a "badder" attitude than mine.

A couple of times, like every time we hear Aaron Carter's voice on the radio, I've lowered the volume even though I heard "but this is my favorite song."

Sure I've made lots of mistakes. And chances are good that I will continue to do so. But wholeheartedly, I try not to make the same ones twice.

I take responsibility for cooking too much food for dinner and for scolding my family for "eating the groceries I just worked so hard to buy!"

And get this, somehow I let my children believe that "You've Got Mail" is a college professor instructing me to sit, by myself for a few minutes, to complete a homework assignment.

But most regrettably, I am guilty of not having asked my mother more questions about her heritage, her troubles, her triumphs, because I was *too busy* to listen to my mother explain her whole life in one sitting.

✳ ✳ ✳

⑦H, THE GUILT !!

(Were we all born with IT, Moms?)

Someday I'll explain to my oldest daughter that when she was just five years old, I forgot to swap a few coins for a newly extracted baby tooth from under the pillow of her sleeping head. (I honestly forgot!)

Worse than that, I'll admit that the coloring books we spotted on the kitchen table the next morning were not from the tooth fairy? ...

And if I'm tortured to confess, I will: "I was mistaken about the entrance age to join soccer, basketball, tennis, Brownies, Irish Step Dancing, horseback riding, opera singing, and drum lessons."

When we better understand 'the situation', we will sit down to write a note to thank a friend named Barbara B. for standing in as 'Tooth Fairy' on that beautiful summer morning. (And about the fairy dust sprinkled about the bed sheets-a day late-I'll take responsibility for that too.)

I'll explain the whole scenario when my girls have youngsters of their own. Gladly!

When children see Angels...

"Before we get into bed, Mom, let's look up to heaven and say goodnight to Grammy. ...Goodnight Grammy. We love you."

"Look Mom! She heard us! Grammy's winking her star at us right now." ...

"We love you too, Grammy!"

Explaining death to my children is one of the most difficult parenting challenges I've been faced with yet. But, thankfully, I know this for sure: *Our loved ones will never be forgotten.* My children wouldn't hear of it. It was those two little girls who encouraged me to talk of my loss and fears. Most of all, to acknowledge our blessings - and Angels!

❋ ❋ ❋

"So I guess if you go up to heaven, you can't come back. Is that right?" Kate asked.

"That's right Kate. You go to heaven when your life on earth is over. But no one who goes to heaven is forgotten. Their friends and family always remember them.

So, in a way, they live on in all of us."

Excerpt from *What's Heaven?* by Maria Shriver

❋ ❋ ❋

"Mommy, are you sad about something?"

"Not really, Elizabeth."

"Then why do you look so funny? Your eyes are all red and stuff. Are you thinking about Grammy?"

"Baby, I think about Grammy all the time, but I know she's safe and happy in heaven."

"Mom, it's not fair that heaven is so far away!"

"No, it's not exactly fair, but that's the way it is Liz. Hey that rhymes," I say to Elizabeth, who doesn't even crack a smile or attempt to change this heavy subject.

"I know that rhymes, Mom. But I'm telling you that it's not fair that we can't see everyone we know who lives in Heaven. Like ever!"

"We have to keep telling them that we love them, Elizabeth. They'll hear us."

"So when I talk to Grammy and tell her we love her, I bet she'll tell Uncle Paul and Auntie M&M and your Nanas and Grandpas, because it's kind of like they all live together now."

In response to her loaded statement, I say, "yes, they do live in heaven, but we should tell them all how much we love them."

"And, Mom, look at all the freckles on my face. That's from all of our Angels sending me kisses. Right?"

"You're right, Elizabeth, and so beautiful with all of the kisses on your cheeks!"

❄ ❄ ❄

"Know what I know, Mommy?" Jackie asks, trying to prove that she too, believes in Angels.

"What do you know, Jackie?"

"I know what 'a' Angel is."

"You do?"

"Yep. She's kind of like a fairy. You know, she has wings and magical powers, but she's almost like a Santa's helper too. She doesn't bring toys for Christmas, but it's her job is to watch us to make sure we do good stuff. Isn't that right, Mommy?"

"Jackie, you are so smart. Our Angels do watch over us. They are a present from God to remind us of the gifts we have, and the ones we'll share tomorrow too!"

"That's almost like what I already said, Mommy!"

"I know!"

When children look sad or frightened...

"I had a bad day on the bus today, Mom."

Looking into her tear swelled eyes I could see that already, but I asked, "Why? What happened, Elizabeth?"

"We had a new bus driver and she got a little lost. She passed my house and I got really afraid. Me and Katie were both crying - just a tiny bit - because the bus passed her house too."

"Why didn't you tell the new driver that she had passed your houses, Elizabeth?"

"Because I was scared. And then a little while later I saw you sitting on the porch and you came running to the bus 'cause you were scared too. Huh Mom?"

"Yes, Elizabeth, I was concerned that your bus was fifteen minutes late." (Actually, I was quite panicked, but 'my look' had told her that already!)

"Well, I'm home now and I promise to tell the driver where my house is next time. That way you won't get so scared again. Okay Mommy?"

"Great, Elizabeth!"

* * *

Mommy, I was really happy at school today until Carson didn't want to play 'blocks' with me. It felt like sand went in my eyes. And then the sand went away when I was playing outside with Bridget and Bryanna and Carson decided he wanted to play 'castle' with all of us. – Jackie

Sometimes, we just need a good cry to cleanse our minds (and the 'sand in our eyes'). Sometimes, we need big ears to hear our tears, and open arms to hug our fears.

A Sensitive Mother

$\mathcal{S}$and In My Eyes

About a year after my mother's death, I (alias, 'Aspiring Writer') gathered the nerve to show up at a "writer's meeting" at a local library.

What a mistake! What did I think to accomplish? The meeting was not comprised of literary agents or publishers. Besides, I was not ready to publish anything anyway. Nor was I ready to share, "really share". I just liked to carry around my notebook and gather thoughts as they arose.

I sat around a table of what I had considered would be ordinary 'wannabe writers' and felt uneasy from the start. Like an intruder from another planet who wrote of simple, straight from the heart kind of stuff. Anyway, this meeting was about sharing, and my turn to "share" came too quickly.

"Jean, would you like to share something please?" I should have said "No thank you, I'm just here to listen." But instead, I fumbled through my papers and plucked from my disarray of notes a very moving poem about life and love and loss. As I began to read, tears formed and uncontrollably splattered on my work. I pinched myself so hard that the self inflicted pain made the tears flow quicker and thicker. Nervous, embarrassed, dreading the silence, I uneasily read another. *(Idiot, you picked the wrong one again!)*

The crowd was quiet while I wiped the dignity from my cheeks. Too quiet. Until finally, one brave listener cleared her throat and spoke, "Wow, you've got a whole lot to say. My advice is for you to go home and take the emotion out of your words - because they definitely say some very important things."

Did she just suggest that I take the emotion out of my writing? *(I'm crushed, utterly flattened.)*

"How does one take the emotion out of her words when she's writing words of sentiment? Answer me that Miss Director of Cold Hearted Affairs?" I whispered to myself.

Miraculously, I gathered the strength to sit through the other member's sharing time.

"Blah, blah, blah, 'Socrates'."

"Blah, blah, blah, 'Euphoria'."

"Blah, blah, blah, blah, blah!"

During the ride home (after I finished blowing my emotions out of a very swollen nose), I began focusing on one of the most rejuvenating, most rewarding, most emotional projects. This piece of work! And then I laughed really hard.

First moral of the story - Never tell a woman not to cry when she needs to (because she will anyway).

Second moral of the story – Never strip naked in front of a bunch of intellectual strangers (unless you're ready for "smart" criticism)!

When children express compassion...

"Mommy, why do mean guys, like the ones on 'bad' movies, have such ugly faces?"

"Well, Jackie, maybe they just have faces that look like they're mad or mean."

"Oh, because they are sad. Right Mommy?"

"That could be, Jackie."

"Know what, Mommy?"

"What, Jackie?"

"Maybe if someone was nicer to them, the 'mean' looking guys might not be sad anymore."

"You're probably right about that, Baby cakes!"

Children, the sensitive little beings that they are, need not be expected to share their parent's more sophisticated emotions. However, when a child expresses compassion and concern -**It's music to my ears!**

* * *

"Mom. Look over there. I think that person is homeless because he has a huge backpack to hold all of his stuff. And he's walking funny, like he lost his shoes too."

I keep my ideals, because in spite of everything, I still believe that people are really good at heart.
Anne Frank
(1929-1945)

"Maybe, Elizabeth, he's walking to the bus station to take a trip and the big bag is filled with lots of his belongings. And perhaps, Elizabeth, his feet are just a little sore."

"Maybe, Mom. But if we see him later, just walking around looking lost, can we give him a pair of daddy's shoes to wear?"

* * *

When children wish....

Can we put a piece of paper on the fridge so we can make a list for Santa, Mommy? It's okay if Santa can't bring everything on the list. He can decide which ones we want the best – or he can just surprise us. Boy, I wish Santa was coming right now!
-Jackie

Dear Santa,
I would like a new bike and Jackie wants a new scooter. And we both like surprises too. Thank you Love, Elizabeth

69

Why do adults equate their worth in relation to the value of their trinkets and expensive toys?

Isn't wishing for life's simple pleasures so much more rewarding?

Let me know when I make you proud.
And help me to have pride in my own accomplishments.
Let me earn your trust. Then trust me.
I won't let you down.
Let me try my wings. If I fail, let me know it's okay.
And encourage me to try again.
Let me know you love me. With a hug. Or a pat on the back.
Or, when I need it,
With a firm but gentle "no."
Let me be. Let me change. Let me grow.
Let me tell you when I'm feeling bad. Or angry. Even at you.
And let me know that even on my worst days, you still like me. Let me dream. Share my joy when my dreams come true. Share my tears when they don't.
Let me feel secure in my home.
Help me realize that love is always there;
that I can depend on you no matter what.
Let me run....let me laugh.....let me play.
And most of all, let me be a child.

Anonymous Poem, from
The Greatest Gifts Our Children Give To Us, by Steven W. Vannoy

When children take risks –
They are on a road to discovery

*Twenty years from now you will be more disappointed
by the things that you didn't do than by the ones you
did do... Sail away from the safe harbor.
Catch the trade winds in your sails.
Explore. Dream.
Discover.*

Mark Twain (1835-1910)

"Jacquelyn, why must you keep spinning around like that? Please, stop it right now!"

"*But, Mommy, I'm just practicing my spinning. Watch me do it real fast. ... Miss Wendy at* Dance Starz Academy (Sagamore Beach) *is 'gonna' be real proud of me!*"

When children take risks...

Mommy, just jump in the ocean. It's not too cold. Your body is just too hot! Watch me and Kylee and Courtney do it first. On your mark, get set, GO!

-Jackie

Children are born risk takers, but for the sake of safety, it's easy to suppress their enthusiasm. After all, we don't want our babies to get hurt!

But think about the alternate ramifications.

When we shield our children from taking any and every risk, we do the opposite of what we attempted to do in the first place.

That's when you'll hear a little voice say, *"Mom, please 'karm' down! I'm only trying new tricks. Maybe you should too?"*

Witness a child spin and twirl
Fearlessly.
Observe a child walk through the snow
Courageously.
Watch a child eat an ice cream cone
Guiltlessly.
Watch a child dunk in the cold ocean
Joyfully.

Amazing, isn't it?
So free of baggage.
So full of enthusiasm and gusto!

❊ ❊ ❊

Witnessing the resiliency and determination of a young child inspires us to mask our fears. And yet, aren't "fear" and "pain" a normal part of life?... Therefore, it is so important to encourage our children to talk through their fears and tend to their pains. But mostly, we must give our children the space to try, and fall, and then try and fall again. Reassuringly! Then listen to a child describe 'courage'.

"You gain strength, courage, and confidence in which you really stop to look fear in the face.... You must do the thing you think you cannot do."
Eleanor Roosevelt
(1884-1962),
"You Learn By Living"

I got a little hurt at recess today. But don't worry, Mom, because Mrs. Johnson, the school nurse, checked that my arm wasn't broken. Then I got back on the swing and started swinging real high. High enough to kick the clouds! -Elizabeth

When children set goals....

"When I grow up,
I want to be ..."
Last year: **A nurse**
Last month: **An astronaut**
Last week: **An actress**
Last night: **A doctor**
This morning: **A veterinarian**
This afternoon: **A tug boat driver**
Tonight: **Post Office**

When my older daughter was "Star of the Week" in her kindergarten class, Elizabeth was asked to complete a form all about her. With Mom's help, she was to list her family members, her most precious belongings, her favorite and least favorite foods, and her goals for the future. Most of the responses I could have filled in with accuracy, except this one:

'What do you want to be when you grow up?'

"Mom, please spell the word 'Post Office' so you can help me write it on that line."

"You want me to spell 'Post Office'? Why is that, Elizabeth?"

"Because that's what I want to be when I grow up."

"Elizabeth, do you mean you want to be a postal clerk, or superintendent of operations, or the treasurer, or a mail delivery person, or the president of USPS? Please explain, so we can fill this out properly."

"Mom, please just spell 'Post Office'. That's it!"

"Okay. But you'll have to tell the class what 'Post Office' means."

"I'm only in kindergarten you know. The kids in my class will definitely understand what 'Post Office' means. So what letter comes after P Mom?"

Truthfully, Elizabeth's response was news to me. She has changed her "when I grow up" vision virtually every week in the past two years. And today, her little sister in training is catching up.

"Jackie, **what do you want to be when you grow up?**" I ask for fun.

"I want to be 'horserider'. That would be a great job! Or maybe I could be a 'French fry cooker' – just like you, Mommy. But I'd really like to work at a zoo. Hmmmm.... I'll tell you what I'm gonna be when I grow up tomorrow, after I dream about it tonight."

"Good morning, Mommy."

"Good morning, Jackie."

"I dreamed about what I want to be when I grow up."

"You did? And what's that, Jackie?"

"When I grow up and turn into a teenager, I want to get a little baby named 'Julesie (next door)' because I love her so so much!!"

✳ ✳ ✳

And then my girls ask me *The Question* that no mother can answer the same way twice.

"Mommy, what do you want to be when you grow up?"

I ponder for a moment.

"Well, besides being a Mom for the rest of my life, I'd like to be a lot of other important things.... like a writer, teacher, grandmother, an award winning chef, and a marathon runner. But for now, I can't wait to be a student again. I can't wait to learn, really learn this time, about: anatomy, geography, social studies, and science. And I am anxious to re-read *Little Women* (and everything else by Louisa May Alcott). Then there will be summer camp, school dances, Midol, first dates, braces, driving school, and senior proms. And oh yes, chaperoning. Lots of chaperoning."

"What's all that stuff mean, Mom? We only asked you what you wanted to be when you grow up."

"I know. And I said I wanted to be a Mother. All of those other things are just important events we'll learn about together."

"Oh."

> *"Life is my college. May I graduate well and earn some honors!"*
>
> Louisa May Alcott
> (1832-1888)

When children make (pinky) promises...

"Mom, you know that a pinky promise is like a lock. Right?"

"Yes it is, Elizabeth. It's a promise that's locked in your heart."

"I know that too, Mom. So let's pinky swear that on my birthday next year, I can have a big party and invite lots of kids to eat pizza and sleep over? And let's promise that we'll love each other forever."

"How about if we just promise each other the love part for now, Elizabeth? Your birthday is not for ten more months and you may change your mind by then about what kind of party we should we plan."

"Good idea, Mom. Here's my pinky!"

Jackie wants to join in on our heart filled, food inspired, birthday related, pinky promise session...

"Mommy, please, on my next birthday, can I have an artist come that can paint faces? Can I have a giant slumber party in the backyard? PLEASE? And I promise that I love you with all my heart too!"

"I think we should just do a pinky promise for loving each other with all of our hearts, because I doubt we'll be having a slumber party in the backyard. Okay Jackie?"

"Ooookkkaaayyyay. Gimmee your pinky please."

✳ ✳ ✳

Here's the best! **A pinky promise combined with a hug.** If we could put words to a child's pinky promise/hug, it would speak of caring reassurance, true love, and fortitude. It's a serious commitment to keep our word. A commitment filled with tenderness – gentle little fingers caressing your heart. AND THEN SOME!!

A Pinky Promise –

Girls, When you learn to read all the words in your fairy tale books, and/or when you realize that there are real villains in our crazy world, I promise to re-read all of your books that I've made up my own endings to these past seven years. Double pinky/hug promise!!

Mom oxoxoxox

A Grown Up Hand Shake –

Parents, I know that it is nearly impossible for busy parents to escape the heavy burdens of adulthood. Okay - more like implausible. But let's make a grown up pinky promise to try. Wholeheartedly! SHAKE, SHAKE, SHAKE....

When children are in search of something ...

Whether a child is looking for her favorite pair of Blue's Clues underwear, the Grandma Nutt card to her Candyland game, a sippy cup filled with her 'bestest' juice, or a hug from her mother, her world revolves around the hunt. Nothing short of natural disaster could stop her from finding what is, at that moment, important.

When my oldest was still crawling, 'binkies' were her most prized possessions. One would never suffice; holding two or three was always better. She was not partial to any one stuffed animal or toy, just to all of them, which actually helped when our search for one thing turned into a hunt for any or every thing.

And then came baby number two. 'Binkies' were gone from the scene in record time but a special pink 'blankie', a gold teddy, a naked dolly, and one particular Barbie were her most favorite things in the world. Actually, they were her world. And so it seems that our days were filled with search parties.

Perhaps the most important lesson I learned from our search parties is this:

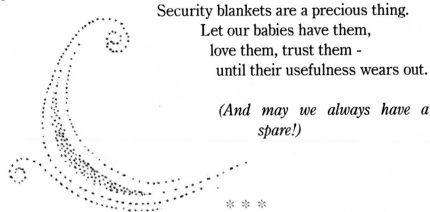

Security blankets are a precious thing.
Let our babies have them,
love them, trust them -
until their usefulness wears out.

(And may we always have a spare!)

* * *

64

And then came the 'Bug Searches' (one of Daddy's favorite pastimes with his girls)

Daddy, don't forget to bring a bucket and a coffee can. We can put the 'rolie polies', like the ones we find under rocks, in the bucket because they can't climb so good. But any of the ones that fly, oh boy, we better catch them in the can! -Elizabeth

And, Daddy, we need some big spoons to dig up the bugs that live under rocks. -Jackie

❊ ❊ ❊

Adult: A stone is nothing but a 'dumb' rock in the dirt!

Child: A rock is the entrance to a world of treasure.

Not only do children have the innate ability to look and really see, they also know how to touch and really feel.

"Mom, want to see something really cool? Check out these worms. ... Hey, where are his eyes?"

"I'm not really an expert on worms, Elizabeth."

"Oh, he doesn't have eyes. He just makes his body feel stuff."

"I think that's possible, but again, I'm not a 'wormologist'."

"Do you want him to crawl on your hand, Mom?"

"Absolutely not!"

"But Mom, he's just a cool little 'wormology' thing!"

> *There is a garden in every childhood, an enchanted place where colors are brighter, the air softer, and the morning more fragrant than ever again.*
> *Elizabeth Lawrence*
> *(1904-1985)*

❊ ❊ ❊

The Beetles and the Bees
By Elizabeth and Jackie

Beetles are kind of boring, but they are still okay to watch.
Fireflies are amazing 'cause they can see in the dark.
Ants are always busy looking for crumbs and digging holes
to hide their food.
Rolly Pollies have cool helmets.
Centipedes can walk around the world if they want to.
Caterpillars are babies.
Butterflies are Moms and she feeds flowers sweet candy.
Moths wish they looked like butterflies.
Ladybugs bring good luck. They have wings and
can fly when they want to.
Spiders know how to sew their own houses.
Mosquitoes bite and make itchy red marks on your skin.
Worms are so cool because they can dig in dirt
or swim in puddles.
Yellow Jackets –
don't ever try to catch one of those crazy things!
Bees make honey, so they must be a little bit good,
but they're dangerous too.

When children trust...

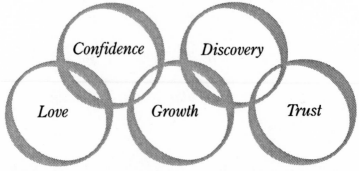

(Kind of like TLC – only a whole lot more passionate)

"Let's read 'The Three Little Pigs' again, Mommy. This time I want to find out where the Momma pig was when the bad wolf tried to huff and puff the little piggys' houses down."

I never considered where Momma pig was, but here goes....

"Well, Jackie, Momma pig might have gone to the store or something. I think the little pigs must have been teenagers or else she wouldn't have left them alone."

"Mommy, she should have been there 'cause her little piggies needed her, even if they were teenager pigs!" Jackie screams.

Elizabeth adds, *"Mom, why would a mother ever leave her children alone when there's a big bad wolf living in the neighborhood?"*

"I don't know much about pigs and such, girls, but I do know that it is a Mom's job to love – and protect – her children."

"Let's read about a different family, Mom. How about this one? It's about a mother holding her baby and then the baby holding his mother when she gets too old to sit up by herself!"

When I held my newborn babies I felt the true meaning of 'Trust.' The essence of that connection between mother and child. A force strong enough to unite us forever.

As our babies grow into toddlers and then preschoolers, they keep reminding us that trust, much like patience, requires practice. Lots of practice!

Yet even on the most difficult of days, we must never break that precious circle of trust, of love. The bond of a lifetime!

"A mother held her new baby and very slowly rocked him back and forth, back and forth, back and forth. And while she held him, she sang:

> I'll love you forever,
> I'll like you for always,
> As long as I'm living,
> My baby you'll be."
>
> From *Love You Forever,* by Robert Munsch

"After we finish reading the story about the baby holding the Momma, I'll go right to sleep because I have my blankie and all my 'amminals' sleeping right over there. But Mom, if I need you, you won't be far. Right?"

"That's a promise Jackie!"

"And Mom, if I wake up in the middle of the night, is it okay if I come into your room to make sure that everything is safe?"

"Of course our home is safe, Elizabeth. Don't forget about Cookie! She can bark really loud when she wants to you know!"

"Oh ya! Cookie and you and daddy won't let anything scary happen around here."

"We try our best!"

"Thanks Mom! I feel safer knowing that."

"You're welcome, Elizabeth."

Before you were conceived I wanted you. Before you were born I loved you. Before you were here an hour I would die for you. This is the miracle of love.
Maureen Hawkins
www.wisdomquotes.com

Ｗhen children make choices...

"I can't decide which movie to watch, Mommy."

"Jackie, please make a choice. Close your eyes and pick one!"

"No, I'll pick one a better way ... Eenie, Meenie, Miny Mo, catch a tiger by the toe. If he hollers let 'em go. Out goes you. My mother told me to pick the 'bess' color of the flag. Red, White, and Blue. ... A B C D E F G H I J K L M N O P Q R S T U V W X Y Z. Okay Mom, I picked one! Let's watch 1000 Dalamashins."

"Do you mean *101 Dalmations*, Jackie?"

"Yep."

※ ※ ※

"Did we use all of the Barbie toothpaste already, Mom?"

"I guess it is gone already, Elizabeth."

"If it's okay Mom, I'll have to use yours."

"Good choice, Elizabeth!"

※ ※ ※

TOO MANY CHOICES:

As it stands right this minute, Tom and I share a tube of ordinary toothpaste which resides on the bottom shelf of the medicine cabinet. But the top of the sink is covered with the children's favorites: Barbie's bubble-fruit, Power Puff Girls' fruity something, SpongeBob's deep sea bubble, and Colgate's newest – mild bubble fruit flavored toothpaste that hums the tune of "ABC's" when the cap is opened.

(How could I resist? Of course the kids will brush harder and longer with this new invention!)

Well, needless to explain...

No more of this nonsense! From now on, I will choose one brand of toothpaste for the four of us, period!

Next trip to the grocery store, I'll perform one of my kids' magic tricks:

> *"Skunk in the barn yard, P.U.*
> *Who put him in there?*
> *Not you.*
> *Skunk in the barn yard, P.U.*
> *Who put him there?*
> *Not you!"...*

And then I will perform some more magic when I'm confronted with the kids preferred juice boxes, their favorite snacks, my husbands choice deli meat, and my personal favorites - whatever makes my life easier dinner entrée choices.

"My mother told me to pick the best one and that one is you!"

※ ※ ※

OLD FASHIONED CHOICES

When I was a child, we had plenty of choices. Take toothpaste, snacks, and playtime for example. We could brush our teeth with Crest (or with baking soda and water). At snack time, we were allowed a piece of fruit or a homemade Popsicle. For fun, we could read Dick and Jane, help mother with her endless chores, or go outside and play.

Sure, we got to watch television occasionally. But our television was not attached to a DVD or VCR player. Nor was it controlled by cable or satellite. We got to watch good old fashioned fun on programs like *Sonny & Cher, Laugh-In, Ed Sullivan, Carol Burnett* (or whatever else my mother chose to watch on one of the four channels that were free of static). And remember those family oriented shows like *Leave It To Beaver, The Partridge Family*, and *The Brady Bunch*. And remember when the Jacksons consisted of five talented boys named Jackson? Remember that? Remember them?

(I'm taking a break now. My favorite show, *Supernanny,* is about to start.)

Motherhood choices

The day you become a
mother is like no other.
There's no going back.
There's no jumping ahead
to Park Place.
But there are many sleep-
less nights, dirty diapers,
temper tantrums, and
diligent three and four
and five and six and seven
year olds to domesticate.
Somehow!?
You could cry, or runaway
and join the circus,
or laugh, and enjoy
the excitement.
You decide.

Fatherhood choices

The day you become a
father, face it guys, you lost
your identity. (Even your
wife calls you 'dad' now.)
Weekend fishing trips are
few and far between.
But there are many games
you can organize, attend,
referee, chauffer, or cater.
Somehow!?
You could work relentlessly,
from sunrise to sunset,
or take a break, and join in
the fun.
(Is it a home cooked meal
or Burger King tonight?)
You decide.

To all of you *Stay At Home Dads* – "HIP HIP HURRAY!" But I Do have one little question:

Why would you name your organization S.A.H.D. - something that sounds so much like the word SAD?

(Sorry. I had to ask! At least I didn't call you *Mr. Mom!* ... You're laughing too. Right?)

"Honey, you gave me some real good advice once, so let me give you some of my own. It's real easy to forget what's important, so don't."

Jack Butler ("Mr. Mom", 1985)

When children grow –
They expand from the inside out

*When I see a baby quietly staring at his or her own hands....or a
toddler off in a corner putting something into a cup and then taking
it out, over and over again...or a preschooler lying in the grass
daydreaming, I like to think that they, in their own ways, are "alone
in the best room" of their houses, using the solitude they need to find
the courage to grow.*

Fred Rogers (1928-2003)

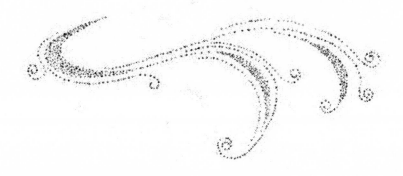

*Nurturing our children's
enthusiasm increases their
spirit for growth.
Read a book together... They'll show you how "big" you
helped them to grow.*

– JML

When children Grow......

"Mom, when we open both eyes and read books - that's what makes our brain and bones grow real big. Me and Jackie read all of these books. Look at our muscles!...Jackie, show Mommy how big your shoulder muscle is now!"

"Wow! You guys are going to be bigger and stronger than me and daddy soon."

"We know, Mom, because we read lots of books."

* * *

Our children's beautiful little bodies manage to grow despite a 3 to 6 year diet consisting of these:

- Frozen bagels, dry Rice Chex and cold Eggos;
- Two orange wedges aside a fluff and peanut butter sandwich;
- Pasteurized cheese atop Blues Clues shaped pasta;
- Chicken fingers, an occasional slice of cucumber and/or 2 cherry tomatoes;
- Ketchup with Tater tots, hot dogs, corn on the cob, pizza, beets, steak, and peas. (Basically, Ketchup with whatever is served for dinner);
- A daily Multivitamin washed down with a fourth of a gallon of 2% milk and Ovaltine.

Amazing, this thing called "growth"!

* * *

And then comes baby number two, who, despite drinking whole milk from bottle nipples that were sterilized via the dish washer (and sucking on binkies that were wiped clean on the inside of Mom's t-shirt), has the ability to grow into a healthy toddler. Baby's precious, palm sized bottom will soon fit into her sister's hand-me-downs - even though she's been swaddled in our arms for way too long! And oh how quickly Baby will tell you that her preference for lunch is not at all the same as her sister's favorite.

Remarkable, this thing called "growth"!

For fun!
A simple technique to entice your children to eat
(or at least try) something new to eat:

Make a small amount of your favorite dish. One of my quick and easy favorites is linguine tossed with olive oil, wine, chicken broth, garlic, grated cheese, and freshly chopped basil and parsley. (But I'll leave out the wine for today's experiment. Use your own discretion on how much, or if, to add the green stuff.)

Cook pasta according to directions. Sauté garlic in olive oil; add remaining ingredients. Simmer for five minutes. Toss with pasta.

Put masterpiece on a small plate; top with grated cheese. Sit down and make announcement,

"Girls, Mommy's just going to relax for a minute and have herself a little snack."

"What Mom? What kind of snack are you having?"

"Oh, just my favorite. If you want to try it, I'll save you a bite. But Mom's real hungry for this masterpiece."

"So are we, Mom. I think we need some more forks!"

My children are so used to seeing green spices in their food, they believe it's the Kitchen Fairy's doing, possibly, because they've heard this so many times before: "Green tasty things in our food are like fairy dust, only edible, because they are so magical and delicious. Now eat up. There are lots of hungry kids in this world!"

Along with a child's physical and emotional development comes their quest for understanding everything...including sexuality...

Mommy, I know we're girls because when we go 'pee', we sit down. But, Mommy, boys have to stand up because they 'pee' out of their bellies! - Jackie

When my oldest daughter was just about three years old, a male friend of ours stopped over for a visit. He excused himself, went into the bathroom, and shut the door - but didn't lock it. Why should he? He's father to three daughters and one son, has very little privacy at home, so why should our house be any different?

"Where's Uncle (full name withheld)?" Elizabeth asked.

"Uncle ......'s in the bathroom. He'll be out in one minute." But my daughter couldn't wait. She was holding the spin wheel to "Twister" and wanted to prove her expertise of the game.

Before Uncle .... could even try to cover up, Elizabeth observed the difference between men and women. The real reason why boys stand up when they go to the bathroom.

Husbands and (bashful) Dads have little choice but to share in The Adventures of Life with Mom and children!

Out of the doorway, Elizabeth ran, screaming, *"MOMMY! DADDY! WHAT WAS THAT? DOES UNCLE .... HAVE A TAIL OR SOMETHING??!!"*

(We've never discussed this again, until now.)

A Tale About Daddy And His Little Girls

With the bat of a few precious eyelashes, children (especially daughters) can convince their parents (particularly their fathers) to do most anything.

"I don't understand why Peter and Tweety don't like me and Lizzy anymore. Every time we try to touch them, they bite our fingers," Jackie sighs.

"Yeah Mom. And every time they do let us take them out of their cage, they run and hide before they try to bite our arms off!" Elizabeth adds.

"We'll just have to talk to Daddy. You both know that he's the expert on bunnies around here."

"Mom, we don't want to sell our bunnies! We just want to trade them for another kind of 'amminal'. Right Lizzy?" Jackie asks, looking for her sister's support.

"Uh huh", Elizabeth answers and adds, *"Me and Jackie really want some kind of pet that we can hold. Like a turtle, or a gerbil, or something cool like that, Mom."*

"Girls, I told you, we'll have to talk to Daddy because he's in charge of the pets in this house."

"Here comes Daddy now!" Jackie screams.

"Jackie, go get Daddy a beer and I'll meet him on the front porch," Elizabeth instructs her younger sister.

"And don't forget Daddy's pretzels. You know how much he loves those," I add to make their plea more convincing. ...

"Hi Daddy. We have something really important to ask you. Actually, Jackie wants to talk to you first. Sit down Dad. Here's your pretzels and beer."

"Wow, Elizabeth, this must be important if you are giving me gifts first," Daddy says with a grin.

While snuggled into Daddy's arms, Jackie completes what her sister started. *"Daddy, you know that our bunnies bite. They even try to bite your arms off when you clean their cage. So can we please trade them in for a nicer kind of 'amminal'?"*

"Please! Please Daddy!?" the girls beg as they shower their Dad with adoring hugs, pouting lips, and flickering eyelashes.

Daddy, in a difficult spot between love and biting bunnies, says, "We'll see girls. I have to make a few phone calls first."

"Let me go get the phone for you, Daddy!"

P.S. *My mother taught me about the power of batting my baby browns too!*

P.S.S. *A trade was recently made. Two 'biting' bunnies for two 'boring' hamsters.*

When Children
Accept Who They Are...

"At daycare today, we were walking out to the playground and everyone was holding hands. I was holding Tony's hand, and know what Mommy?"

"What, Jackie?"

"His hand is a different color than mine, but it was just the same size! Isn't that so cool?"

"That is really cool, Jackie!"

"And Mom, know what?"

"What, Elizabeth?"

"I have kids in my class who can't do 'Bradley' as good as most of us can. But that's okay, because they'll learn better when they go into a quieter room and listen to special tapes."

"That they will, Elizabeth."

"And Mom. If I ever have to stay after school to learn something extra, would that be alright?"

"That would be fine, Elizabeth."

"Good, because I think I need a little help with my math family facts."

It's refreshing to observe a child's approach to life - without prejudice or pretense. They readily accept that everyone is born with unique needs, strengths, and weaknesses.

I love you just the way you are!

Fred Rogers
(1928-2003)

 Best of all, our children know that they are meant to be loved for who they are, not for who we want them to be.

* * *

"Hey Mom. Look at Dad's lobster boat. Your name is on there. It's like you're really famous now!"

"I know. I sure have made it to the big time!"

"Are you going to work on Daddy's boat and hold the fish heads too, Mom?"

"Let's hope not girls!"

"But Mom. You might have to! What if Daddy's helpers don't want to go to work someday? Daddy still has to go fishing you know, and he can't do it by himself."

YIKES!

* * *

Once we joined the ranks of motherhood, isn't it amazing all the things that we accept as normal?

Your name on your husband's assets, Boo-boo bunnies, sippy cups, tardiness, play groups, Chuckie Cheese, training wheels, formal play rooms, and minivans..........

About The Cars We Drive

"Mom, look! There's a girl driving her daddy's big truck."

"Jackie, just because a girl is driving a truck doesn't mean she's driving her dad's truck."

"Yes sa! Mommy."

"No sir! Jacquelyn."

"Mom, you don't drive a truck."

"No, I drive a minivan."

"That's what I mean. Our dad drives a truck and you drive a van. And Annie's Mom drives a van and her dad drives a truck. All Moms drive vans!"

"Not all, but many of the moms we know do drive vans, Jackie."

"So Mom, that girl's van must be broken and that's why she had to drive her dad's truck."

"Or maybe, Jackie, that girl just wants to drive a truck." (PAUSE)

"Well, maybe. ... But I don't think so."

* * *

When children create masterpieces out of ordinary things...

"I used Daddy's fishing boxes to make a house for the little dollies who used to live in the toy box. Then I used this carpet – actually it's just a towel - to fly them to the store. Wouldn't that be a great way to drive to the candy store, Mom?"

"Who knows, Jackie. Maybe we will be able to take a magic carpet ride to the store some day."

"That would be so cool! I 'hosey' I get to ride in the front!"

Every child is an artist.
The problem is how to remain an artist once he grows up.

Pablo Picasso
(1881-1973)

* * *

"Can you buy me a diary, Mom, so I can write down all the important things I do? Here's a story, about all of us having a family day at 'Ventur Il'."

"That's wonderful work Elizabeth! Does this spell 'Adventure Isle'?"

"Yes Mom. Even if I can't spell all the words perfectly, I can sound them out and make pictures too. Here's me on the water bumper car."

Children express themselves through their artwork. They are proud of their efforts and expect them to be displayed. All of them! (Take **Refrigerator Art** for example!)

"Mommy, can we hang this picture of a zebra I made for you on the refrigerator?"

"Sure we can, Jackie. That way, every time we glance towards the refrigerator, we can admire it, and your school calendar, and your preschool pictures, and all of Lizzy's calendars, school pictures and drawings, and photos of Grammy, and Auntie Be's pot-roast recipe, and Auntie Lisa's smiling face, and the snapshot of Auntie Ellie and her dog, and the picture of Cookie, our dog, chasing the lawnmower, and the photograph of Daddy's boat, and the portrait of you and Jake at the Children's Museum, and the image of you when you were in my belly.".........

"Here Mom, I think you need some more magnets to hold everything on the fridge."

"Thank you. Jackie, can you count to 100 yet?"

"Well, almost. I can try to do it."

"Good. We'll practice today when you help to pick the 'refrigerator art' off the floor."

"Great!"

PSSST.......

Parents,

When you're rearranging (i.e., recycling) your children's art-work, be sure to place yesterday's drawings in a discrete place. Just remember, children have x-ray vision and can see through most <u>sgab fo hsart</u>. *(The underscored were intentionally spelled backwards in fairy language, and may require reading in the reflection of a mirror).*

✳ ✳ ✳

If I were an inventor:

...I'd invent refrigerator magnets that hold 10+ papers at once for 10+ minutes at a time.

...I'd (re)invent things that reinvent themselves, like play dough and paper dolls.

...I'd invent a one multipurpose wipe that can handle it all (faces, butts, spills, germs, ovens, dogs, toilets, ceilings, etc.)

....I'd invent rainbow colored stick-its on a roll. I'd call it "Say It and Display It" and I'd do just that, everywhere!

...I'd invent a new clock. One that adds two hours of ME TIME to every day!

✳ ✳ ✳

When Children Learn Something New...

"Hey Mom, did you know that D.A.D. spells DAD both ways?
"It sure does, Elizabeth. Forward and backwards."
"And do you know what W.O.W. spells, Mom?"
"Yes, it spells WOW."
"Right. Now sound out what M.O.M. spells?"
"It spells MOM."
"Now write your name, not your real name but your 'Mom' name and then turn the whole page upside down.... Isn't that so cooooool? MOM spells WOW, sort of!"
"Lizzy, you are so right. MOM does spell WOW, sort of. Thank you for teaching me that."

Mom spells wow

∗ ∗ ∗

Children encourage us to look at the very obvious with curious eyes as they prove that we are never too young to begin - or too old to continue - learning.

Mom, please pick up the computer disks like this, with one finger, or else you'll ruin the game with your germs. I want to show you how to make Arthur's tree house. It's not magic. You just have to learn to click on the right things. Watch me first. – Jackie

What's that they said about 'old dogs and new tricks' – or it is 'old tricks and new dogs'?...

"The child sees everything with new eyes. Something we have lost along the way because it is safer to fit in. Many so-called different people we admire are not unique. It is merely the way they have chosen to expand their minds and souls rather than retract them..."

From the article *"You Can Teach An Old Dog New Tricks"*
by Loretta LaRoche

News flash in the car. (Always in the car!)

"Oh Mom, I forgot to tell you about something that happened at school."

"What is it, Elizabeth?"

"Just check in my back pack when we get home. I put a note in one of the pockets, from the Principal of the school, to tell you to check my head real good."

"Elizabeth, what am I checking your head for?"

"I'm not sure. But someone in my class has head 'ICE' or some kind of bugs living in there."

"What!? Did you say head lice???"

"Yes. But don't worry about me, Mom. The nurse checked my head real good – like every piece of my hair - and she said I could come back to school on Monday."

"Oh, well that's good."

"And know what else Mom?"

"What, Elizabeth?" I ask, awaiting more newsworthy information.

"We were on the bus, and remember those boys I showed you at the playground the other day?"

"Yes."

"Well, those boys told the bus driver that me and Samantha were chasing them and that we were trouble starters. So the bus driver told us we couldn't sit near the boys anymore."

"Elizabeth, did you girls start trouble with the boys?"

"No Mom! We were just telling the boys to stop chasing us at the park. Remember they were doing that?"

"Yes, but I thought you were just playing Tag."

"While you were sitting down and talking to the other Moms, the boys were chasing us because they were trying to kiss me and Samantha! Mom, did you hear me?"

"Yes, Elizabeth. I heard you loud and clear."

"Well?"

"You should stay away from those boys on the bus, at school, and at the playground. Okay Baby?"

"Fine. We don't want to kiss those stinky boys anyway! Yuk!"

When children bond with loved ones and friends...

"Mom, we have a really big family and everyone loves us so much. You and Daddy love us more, because we're your kids. But our Aunties and Uncles and Nana and Grandpas said they love us with their whole hearts. It's almost like they wish we were their kids!"

"That's because, girls, you are their kids too!"

When family and friends connect with our children, they enhance our lessons about love. Real love....

"Mom, did God make me your kid because you wished really hard for me? And did I get a sister after we all wished really hard together?"

"Elizabeth, Daddy and I wished and prayed for you, and for Jackie too. And our prayers were answered."

"I'm glad, Mom, because it would be pretty boring playing 'house' without Jackie."

"Lizzy is my big sister and big sisters can be best friends too. Right, Mommy?"

"Actually, Jackie, sisters should be best friends. Look at me and Auntie Lisa."

"She is your 'bestest' sister-friend. Right Mom?"

"That she is, Jackie!"

*Watching my girls is like reliving the days of
'Me and Lisa'; the 'Twinkle Eyes and Sweetie
Face Show'. It's amazing!
The similarities and differences;
The quarrels and agreements;
The laughter and tears;
The love between two sisters.
Best friends forever!*

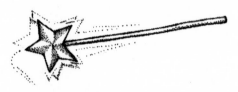

Some friendships were just meant to be

Last summer, at the season's first swimming lesson, my girls discovered the obvious: somebody else's mother brought the best snacks to the beach (and enough of them for the whole swim team to enjoy).

"Girls! Time for lunch," I call from our blanket. My daughters ignored me as they snuggled themselves in their friends towels, helped themselves to their snacks, and played with their beach toys. Jackie was even wearing one of the other girl's water slippers.

Mortified, I called my girls again. "JACQUELYN AND ELIZABETH!" They heard me this time.

"Please Mom? Can we eat with our new friends? They brought double stuffed Oreos for lunch and you only brought ham sandwiches," my girls chant in duet.

The other mother, infringing upon my "Me" minutes, enthusiastically asks of me, "Hey, Jackie and Liz's Mom, come and join us. We're having a picnic."

Reluctantly, I drag all of our belonging to join the gang.

"Hi, I'm Michelle. These are my girls, Bella, Sophia and Juliette. What's your name, besides Jackie and Liz's MOM?" Michelle asked of me.

"That is my real name these days, 'Momma Jeana', but my alias is Jean. ..."

During lunch, Michelle and I learn a whole lot about one another and the time in the sun passed too quickly.

"Girls, we have to go now because I have to go to work for a little while."

"Oh, you have to go to work?" Michelle asked and continued with the questions:

"Where's that?"

"Are you coming back to the beach in the morning?"

"If you have to work tomorrow afternoon, maybe the girls could stay here with us and I'll bring them home by 3?"

"Don't you live in the .... house on .... Street?"

The kids overheard the question and answer session.

"Tomorrow, you don't even have to make our lunch, Mom. Just bring us to the beach and this nice lady (what's your name again?) can feed us. And after we're done playing at the beach, Bella and Sophia and Juliette's mom will bring us home."

Michelle laughs and adds, "Here's my phone number. Call me tonight so we can make a play date."

> *My kids – and my Mother – are right. We can never have too many friends.*

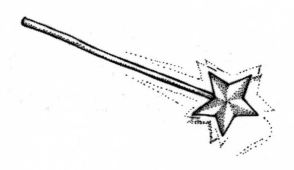

More About Bonding ...

"Mom, can I write a note to Tina? I haven't seen her in a long time and I want to tell her what I've been doing."

"Sure we can, Elizabeth."

"Why don't they send us cards or email or anything anymore? Tina was like my first best friends too! "

"I know that Elizabeth, and Tina's mother was one of my first best friends too! So, let's send another note today."

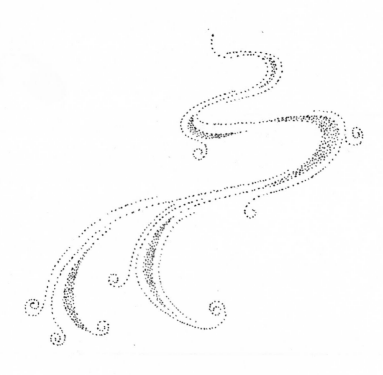

When children live the 'Now' of each day – They show us the way

* * *

Today is your day!
Your mountain is waiting.
So... get on your way.

Dr. Suess (1904-1991)

* * *

"This is funny, Mom. It's like we woke up in the morning and then blinked our eyes and now it's already time to go to bed."

"Isn't it funny, Elizabeth, how quick times flies when you're having a good time?"

"Actually, it's not really funny Mom. It's like the time just flew away!"

"Wait a few years, Elizabeth. You'll see how quickly time really does fly."

"No thanks."

When children live the 'Now' of each day...

What are we gonna do (first) today? It sure is a beautiful day for the ponies – at the horse farm – to eat our carrots. – Jackie

"Hey everybody, look outside! It's starting to snow! That means today is a great snowman making day. – Elizabeth

Children wake every morning with recharged batteries and a refreshed zest for life. They open their eyes and it starts.
The questions, the goal setting, the prioritizing of unlimited fun to be had during the course of each new day.
Here we go again!

Our children are mastering the art of living through optimism, are growing in resiliency, and 'live the moment' every minute of their waking day.
If we listen to the whispers... from the 'mouth of our Babes'... we can too!

✳ ✳ ✳

More about *Time*, which is *always* on *their* side:

Teaching our children the notion of telling time is at the top of a mother's list of 'Difficult Concepts to Explain.' Young children simply do not understand abstract concepts of time, such as "soon" or "later". Forget about correlating hours into days and days into a week, month, or calendar year. So how can a child possibly comprehend the birthday party they were invited to is exactly 12 days and 6 hours away?

"Mommy, Auntie Lisa told me we're going to Cousin Johnny's birthday party in twelve days. We're gonna see Baby William too, so can I please pick out the dress I want to wear 'the next day'?"

"Not just yet, Jackie. Let's call Auntie Lisa so she can better explain exactly when we will see your cousins."

"Okay, but let me get my dress ready first!...And Mom?"

"What Jackie?"

"Don't forget about my other cousins (Jessica, Katie, Tara and Mikie). They have birthdays soon too you know."

Take it from me:
It makes perfect sense to keep surprises,
calendars, and clocks as Mommy's tools,
for no other reason than it's just easier.
(Got it Auntie Lisa?)

* * *

And yet...

Isn't 'NOW' the perfect time for all things we forgot -or were too busy - to do and say yesterday?

Where's the telephone?
Where are those cards I meant to mail last week?
Where's that recipe for homemade play dough?
What time does the the Barnstable County Fair open anyway?

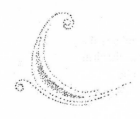

* * *

The real meaning of 'NOW' –
It's all about spending the time
making precious memories!

Another busy day *In the Life of Mother with Children* is upon of us.....

We're dressed, our teeth are brushed. Buttered toast is wrapped in paper towels and we're safely strapped into our seats in record time. I maneuver our minivan into a drive-through line, crowded with fifteen other minivans, to get my morning dose of caffeine.

Jackie takes a bite of her toast and surmises the situation.

"Mommy, this is a really cool coffee place. Look at all the pictures. Wow! They have ice cream here too. I know we can't have ice cream with our toast for breakfast, but Mom, can we please get one of those icy drinks 'cause we forgot to drink our juice at home?"

Liz adds, *"I'd like a red one please."*

We left the house in a rush, so I give in and order two (expensive) frozen drinks along with my coffee.

Jackie puts her straw into her cup, takes a sip, and asks Elizabeth, *"Isn't this 'sludge' great?"*

"Yep! Are we almost to the fair yet Mom?"

"Not quite. A little while longer girls."

"Elizabeth! Look over there. It's Lizzie McGuire. She's in that big white 'limbo'."

"Jackie, that's not Lizzie McGuire. Besides, Hilary Duff drives in a black limo, not in a white 'limbo'."

"Oh."

And so they chat for the remainder of the ride. I drive – and listen to my babies grow up. ...

"Mom, look! There's the Barnstable County Fair! Please park the car right here, so we can be there already!" Elizabeth howled from the backseat.

"Yeah Mommy, hurry! We have to see the sheep before they get all their hairs cut off! I think there's gonna be a zebra here too!" Jackie added to the excitement.

"Okay, okay, we're here! Last one to the gate is a rotten egg!" I screamed without hesitation.

When children sleep......

Fact #1: They dream about today - which seemed to end before they had a chance to do, well, most everything on their endless list of to do's.

Fact #2: They fantasize about tomorrow – the best parts anyway.

How do our children have the ability to store every syllable spoken to them, from sunup to sundown, in their awesome memory bank? Then, at bedtime, they have the capability to download each and every word:

"But Mom, you said we could make brownies today."

"Remember we talked about going to the mall today?"

"You said we could to have a tea party after dinner!"

"And what about finger painting with our feet? Today was definitely a finger painting with our feet day, Mommy!"

It's not that a mother's memory bank is not as awesome as her child's. It's just that our computers are (so often) on overload.

Don't you wish your brain had extended and expanded RAM capabilities (like you know who)?

Night time silliness

It's 7:39 p.m., twenty one minutes till our curfew, when I announce, "Kids, time to clean up and get ready for bed." Those few words turn two tired little girls into energizer bunnies who attempt to accomplish everything and anything in the next however long they can.

"But Mommy, we're not tired! We can't go to bed yet because our movie just started and we haven't seen Mary Poppins clean the kids' room with her magic," Jackie says.

"And Mom, I just have to finish this beautiful picture I'm making for you. I only have this (huge) pile of crayons to use till I'm done. It won't take long. Besides, I haven't brushed my teeth yet," Elizabeth adds.

Once you've convinced the children that it is indeed "CLEAN UP TIME", it happens. Every toy that is touched, moved, lifted, nudged, or breathed upon, comes alive:

Barbie's CD player blares "London Bridge is Falling Down"
Ernie snores and belts out "I Feel Great"
Woody yells "Howdy Partner"
Barney's guitar strums "I Love You"
Scooby Doo yells "RutRo" and Shaggy screams "Yikes!,
A telephone rings and the Operator announces "9-1-1,
What's your emergency?"
A little Chinese doll sings "It's a Small World"
And something else, (I still haven't figured out what)
starts singing "Old MacDonald Had a Farm".

The kids ask, *"Mommy, Daddy, isn't this fun?"*
But Mommy and Daddy know that it's fifteen minutes past having a good time...

* * *

"Goodnight, girls.
I love you with all my heart, just because you are so smart!
Sweet dreams."
"Goodnight, Mom. We love you too. (PAUSE) But we just have to tell you one more thing."
"What is it girls?" I ask, awaiting the final dissertation of the day.
"Mommy, know what?
"What, Jackie?"
"When we go to sleep tonight, we'll dream about everything about today."

"And Know what else, Mom?"

"What, Elizabeth?"

"We'll dream about tomorrow too!"

"Well girls, I hope you have happy dreams about today – and tomorrow too! And I know you'll wake in the morning raring to go. Ready to be loved and listened to, just like you did today, and yesterday, and all the days before that."

Twinkle, twinkle, little stars...

Once my girls have been tucked in and all is quiet, I tiptoe back into their room to see my dreaming angels. I sit by their beds, watch them, and think about our busy day.

These little beauties couldn't possibly be the ones who "by a accident" squeezed a whole tube of Rugrats toothpaste onto 2 little toothbrushes just minutes ago? And it couldn't have been these snoring cherubs who rearranged every little thing in Mommy's crowded walk-in closet this afternoon? Never! They are too precious. They are too adorable and sweet.

Gently moving strands of moist hair from their foreheads, I sit longer, fantasizing about their dreams.

Just as I thought:
Tomorrow will be as full of nonsense,
and promise,
as the days before!

When children make the rules...

In a world where children rule,
every day would be a holiday.

"Mommy, when it's my birthday, can I please have my birthday at one of those cool party places where Eva and Richard had their birthday? And don't forget the goody bags!"

"Well Jackie, remember what I said about your birthday? Based on the way you've been acting today, there will be no party!"

"But Mom, we have to have my birthday, even if I wasn't extra good today!"

"And why is that, Jackie?"

"Because, Mommy, my birthday will still come!"

"I know that Jackie, but that doesn't that mean a party necessarily comes with it."

"I promise to be good, every minute till my birthday Mommy. How many days away is it anyway?"

"About 120 days."

Who invented "Goody Bags" anyway? Why are they necessary? Why are they the best part of a birthday party? And why are children so obsessed about their next birthday? Please, I need some answers!

Mommajeana1@aol.com

"Oh. That means it's not tomorrow or the next week?"

"That's right Jackie, but you promised to be good every day till then. Remember?"

"I know Mom, I will. How many days is that again?"

✳ ✳ ✳

Think about the power of a birthday to a child. It is her day to be the star! A day when the party girl's friends give her gifts before they enjoy a sliver of her awesome 'Barbie' cake. And in her heart, the birthday girl knows the day is all about her. Totally! Without guilt!

※　※　※

"Jackie, when it's your 5ᵗʰ birthday, guess what kind of present I want to give you?"

"Elizabeth, my next birthday is not my 5ᵗʰ."

"Yes it is, Jackie. You already had your 4ᵗʰ birthday; that means your next birthday will be your 5ᵗʰ."

"No 'sa! I'll be my 'five birthday', not my 5ᵗʰ. Besides Elizabeth, 5ᵗʰ is part of a dance called a plie'. Watch me do it….."

"Oh brother!"

"Elizabeth, I'm not your brother! Silly!! I'm your sister!!!"

And then comes Christmas, that wonderful season to celebrate in so many ways!

"Lizzy, today is Christmas Eve. Isn't that great? That means Santa comes to our house in just three more days."

"Jackie, Christmas Eve means Christmas is tomorrow! It means Santa comes to our house tonight!"

"Wow. So we should make our Santa cookies now!"

"Yep."

"Momma! Are you ready to make Santa's cookies?"

The Daily Gift

You know what?
Tomorrow is a new day.
And today is a new day.
Actually,
Every day is a new day.
Thank you, God,
For all of these
Special and new days.

From *Heartsongs*, by Mattie J.T. Stepanek,
(July 17, 1990 – June 22, 2004)

＊ ＊ ＊

Motherhood is teaching me where to get the strength to approach every day as if it were my first, or last. As difficult as that may be to think about, THINK ABOUT IT, and then ask yourself these questions:

If you knew today would be your 'last day',
Would you do things differently?
Would you say things differently?
Would you see things differently?
Would you hear things differently?
(Remember, honesty counts!)

When children are children –
They expect these precious moments to be savored

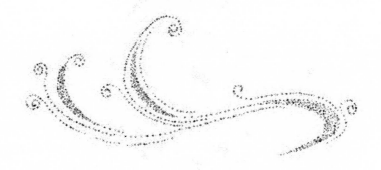

You too, my mother,
Read my rhymes,
For love of forgotten times,
And you may chance
To hear once more
The little feet along the floor.

Robert Louis Stevenson (1850-1894)

About my childhood, you ask?
I'm living it all over again!
                    The Author

When children are Children...

Mommy, keep your cheek still and pretend my eyeballs are a butterfly and I'm kissing you with my wings. - Jackie

✳ ✳ ✳

"*Mom, can we just lie together and talk about things for awhile?*"

"Sure we can, Elizabeth. What do you want to talk about?"

"*Well, now that I'm in first grade that means I get to stay at school for a long time. It's like I'll be gone from breakfast till dinner. Of course I'll be home for dinner, but when I'm in high school, I won't have to be home until bedtime. Right Mom?*"

"Not exactly, Elizabeth. Dinner will be served in this house every night at the same time - and no matter how old you are, I'll expect you to be here with clean hands and a day full of events to discuss."

I hope to never have to ask my children to share their thoughts -or butterfly kisses!

"*But Mom, of course I'll be home for dinner, because you're the best cook I know. You even cook better than McDonalds, except their big kid meals are pretty awesome.*"

"Thank you, Elizabeth, for the half compliment."

"*What does that mean Mom?*"

"It means I appreciate half of what you said."

"*Does that mean I only get half of a dessert tonight?*"

"No. But if you say the same thing when you're sixteen it may," I add with a smile.

"*That's funny Mom,*" *Elizabeth beams back.*

✳ ✳ ✳

Listen to our children so candidly reinforce the truth –
*Every time we are not fully engaged in the moment, it is time we
have lost forever.*

❄ ❄ ❄

"Can we look at our books of pictures, Mom?"
"Sure we can, Jackie."
*"Here's me when I was one years old…. Here's Elizabeth when she
learned to eat spaghetti…. Here's me and my backpack going to the
first day at Rainbow school….Here's all of us playing at the beach…..
Oh Mom, look at this one. It's you holding Elizabeth and me when I
was just born. I bet you wish you could still hold us like that."*

"Jackie, you girls are much too big to carry like babies now, but
we can cherish those memories in our hearts."
"Cool."

---

*Think about it. No more Christmas presents out
of toothpicks and library paste. No more sloppy
oatmeal kisses. No more tooth fairy. No giggles in
the dark. No knees to heal, no responsibility. Only
a voice crying, "Why don't you grow up?" and the
silence echoing, "I did."*

*From "No More Oatmeal Kisses" by Erma
Bombeck (1927-1996)*

When children are the students...

"Know what we're learning all about at (Ella F.) Hoxie (Elementary) School, Mom?"

"What Elizabeth?"

"Respect, kindness, and safety."

"That's great. Tell me more."

"Well, respect means being nice, not touching other kid's things, and saying 'thank you' when someone gives you something. And kindness means the same thing. Sort of," Elizabeth adds, breathes, and then continues.

"Kindness definitely means being nice to other people and not ruining anyone else's things. And safety means not getting 'ourselfs' into trouble, like making sure we look both ways before we cross a street. And safety means being careful not to kick anyone when we climb on the monkey bars. But if we do see anyone get hurt, we should try to help them. Safety means a lot of things, Mom!"

"It sure does, Elizabeth."

"And Mom, Ms. Haskell, our Principal, comes in and talks to our class about all of this, like almost every day. Sometimes she even has assemblies where the whole school listens about safety, respect, and kindness. And then we go back to our classroom with Ms. Costello and draw and write it."

"How awesome, Elizabeth. Your teachers want to make sure everyone understands that respect and kindness and safety are important qualities of life."

"She didn't say they were 'qualtees' of life, Mom. Ms. Haskell said that we should behave safe and kind and nice, even when we're not at school."

"That's because, Elizabeth, Ms. Haskell knows that it's all about thinking with your head and listening with your heart!"

"Well, I definitely know how to stop, look, listen, and be nice too, Mom, because we hear all about it every day!" | *Way to go*

Hoxie!

SCHOOL'S OUT FOR THE SUMMER!

No more rush to meet the school bus. No more hurry to get the best parking spot at preschool. No more discussions about what to wear to school and no more early morning confrontations about the "fun" things we'll do afterwards. Now what?

I gather the girls for a Mother/Daughter discussion. "Girls, what do you want to do this summer?"

"Well Mom," Elizabeth answers as if she's going into high school instead of second grade, *"The summer goes by so quick; we should just have fun. And I hope we don't have to have babysitters, because you and Daddy deserve a summer break too ya know!"*

"And Mom," Jackie adds as though she'll be teaching, rather than attending, kindergarten. *"I just wanna do all the great summer stuff that kids do with their Moms and Dads - and skip daycare."*

That did it. My children touched my self-employed heart like never before. I have to call Tom and talk about this.

"Tom, please call the broker. Tell him our restaurant is free for the next available taker. Tell him we need a little break while our girls are still so young and playful! They just told me they want to have fun with both of us this summer, so what do you say? Let's go camping, fishing, for long walks along the canal and then out for ice creams in our p.j.'s. Tom, we only live once you know! They are only kids for a very short time you know! Oh Tom, this is going to be a great summer"......

Elizabeth Lanahan graduated from first grade, and our guess is that she will spend her summer swimming and searching for sea creatures. Jacquelyn Lanahan recently wore her Preschool cap and gown, and odds are great that she will spend her summer doing what kids do best. Being a kid! Jean and Tom Lanahan recently "leased" their adolescent (their 12 year old restaurant, that is). Rumor has it that Jean will spend her summer days playing at the beach, waving toward the sea - to her smiling, oilskin clad husband.

"Tom? Are you there? Hello? HELLOOO?"

"What did Dad say, Mom?"

"Oh, his cell phone seemed to be out of range. We'll talk to him about it when he gets home."

When children receive rewards (and give gifts)...

"Mom, come look! I cleaned out my 'artist' bucket and threw away all the markers that don't write anymore."

"Wow. Nice job, Elizabeth!"

"Can we make a chart that shows how I organize my art things so then I'll get 'llowances? What is 'llowances anyway? Is it money or new toys or something?"

"Allowances, Elizabeth, are special privileges that parents give to their children for helping with the chores."

"So can we make a clean up chart and put stars on there when we do extra special chores for you, Mom?"

"Sure we can."

"And can we hang it on my door so everyone will see what a good helper I am?"

"Absolutely."

"And when the chart is full, can I get a dollar or something, because that's what I thought allowances would be, Mom?"

"How about fifty cents, Elizabeth?"

"Okay. Let me get some stars ready and you can get some money ready. Now, what chores do you want me to do first, Mom?"

"How about if you scrub the marker scribbles off your desk? Here's a clean cloth. Make sure you put some elbow grease into it!"

"Mom! This is hard work. See all the elbow grease on my cloth.
I should get a lot of stars for doing this dirty chore! Maybe when the
chart is full of stickers, Mom, you could give me some of the 'college
dollars' that Uncle Peter always sends to us? Oh, never mind, because
I don't think I can buy candy with that kind of funny money!"

"You're right, Elizabeth. So let's stick to quarters for now."

✳ ✳ ✳

Look at this present we got from Auntie Pattie and Uncle Jimmy in
Florida. Let's take out all the pretend food pieces and cooking things
so we can jump and play in the squishy stuff? This is the best box we
ever got!

-Elizabeth and Jackie

Huge, little rewards

I can say this now, perhaps with more authority since my
children sleep through the night (most of the time); get themselves dressed (when they are in a rush); and pour milk into their
cereal bowls (if they insist upon it enough):

As demanding and challenging, and tiring and
poor paying as "our job" is, Motherhood is also the
most rewarding vocation!

If you need to be reminded of this, think about the moment you
held your newborn and she instantly recognized you as the one
who fed her chili the last nine months.

And remember when your toddler told you she loved you,
'really lubbed you' while you were in the middle of complaining
about Legos scattered under your every step?

How about when your child knew you were having 'a moment'
and your little one brightened your spirits by making you a
dandelion bouquet?

105

Here's the best: In the midst of it all, witnessing your child hug a sibling, share a chocolate chip cookie with her teddy bear, clean up her own mess, or willingly give away her favorite things.

Those are moments that camouflage the challenges associated with motherhood. Those are instances that encourage us to continue to try our best. Those are simple little rewards that don't have a dollar sign in front of them (and never will). Those are occurrences that validate one of my mother's favorite sayings, **"What goes around, comes around!"**

Mommy, can I give my favorite pink boots to Molly? She's just a baby - and babies don't have any boots you know. - Jackie

I have another 'Bratz' doll almost like this one, so I want to give it to Shannon because she loves 'Bratz'. Probably as much as I do! - Elizabeth

And then there are the extra-special gifts, given straight from the hearts of our Babes.

Here's a star I made for you Mommy. - Jackie

I made this card for you. Actually, I copied the letters from another card, because I liked what it said, but this one is special - just for you Mom! - Elizabeth

> Happy Mother's Day, mommy. mommy. may all your Mothers Day wishes come true, and I hope this will be a happy one for you. With Love and kisses On Mother's Day Love. Elizabeth Lanahan

If you ever doubted that greeting cards are not worth sending, come to our house where cards have a home in the drawers of a desk in our family room. (Hallmark should pay us board!) Now that my kids are learning to spell, and read, and write, they do just that, word for word, over and over again.

(Isn't that the reason we send cards in the first place?)

The greatest gifts to give and receive

I am learning what a Mother expects of her daughters.
I would be totally satisfied if my daughters treasure our lessons – and our relationship - forever and a day.
And I am well aware of what a daughter expects of her Mother...I pray that I achieve what my mother accomplished.

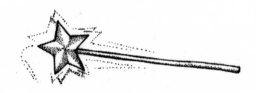

To

Elizabeth and Jacquelyn,

This book is for you,
Baby Girl - times two!
It's a reflection of today -
To thank you in special way
For all the joy you bring;
the precious songs you sing!
For the many Fairies you know,
And all the enchantment they sow!

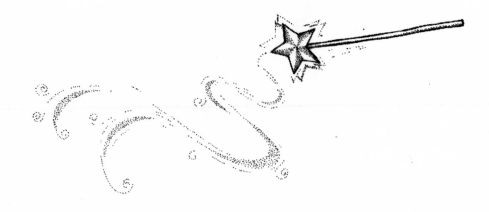

When children role play, We see our own reflections in the mirror

We never know the love of a parent until we become parents ourselves.
Henry Ward Beecher
(1813-1887)

"Mirror, Mirror, on the wall, who's the fairest of 'em all?"
Elizabeth asks of me.

Looking into my reflection, I answer, "Why you, Miss Elizabeth, are the fairest of them all - because you are my oldest daughter."

"What about me Mom?" Jackie asks.

Looking into my likeness, I answer, "Why you, Miss Jacquelyn, are the fairest of them all also - because you are my youngest daughter."

When children role play ...

Teach a child a song and a few dance moves and then watch your 'little me' perform. Listen to her verses. Witness her pirouettes. It's enlightening, yet a little frightening at the same time. As if we're looking in the mirror and seeing our young selves - past, present, with future promise - all intertwined in a new little body.

And parents, may we take a closer look....

This is our opportunity to keep what worked and to fix what was broken from our repertoire of childhood lessons.

"Mommy, even when you get really old, like 50, will you still be my Mommy?

"I'll be your Mommy until the end of time, Jackie, even when I'm 50."

"That's good, because I think I'll always need a Mom."

"And Mom, when you get really old, like a little older than 50, will I have two girls just like you have me and Jackie?" Elizabeth asks.

"I hope you have children someday, but please wait until I'm really old. Okay baby?"

"Mom, I am not a baby! I'll be nine on my next birthday."

"I know, and I'll only be 44."

"So Mom, when I have a real baby, someday I mean, she will be your baby too. Right?"

> My daughter's daughter is my daughter twice over.
>
> *A Greek Saying*

"That she will. And know what else, Elizabeth?"

"What Mom?"

"She'll be a reflection of you. And I'll love her, **always and forever, with my whole heart and soul,** just as I love you and Jackie, **my pride and joy**!"

"Cool. But, Mom, maybe we should name my baby something different than 'pride and joy' - because that's what you call me and Jackie."

"I'll let you decide on that one, Elizabeth."

---

*Oh my! Those phrases -***always and forever, whole heart and soul, my pride and joy*** *- were my mother's words first! (S... ! It's happening, just like my mother always told me it would! And there's no going back now!)*

That means tomorrow I will be saying things like:

"Mark my words"

"Just wait"

"Finish your supper or else..."

"When you have a baby of your own!"

＊ ＊ ＊

Been there, done that feelings

Is Deja Vu a reflection of our experiences? Or is it an ability to see similar situations through new lenses?

The other day I brought my girls to one of their play groups (i.e., to the babysitter's house) and I stayed around for a little while, to observe.

YaYa greeted me, looking bright - like she had had her morning fill of coffee. The dish cloth hanging over her shoulder proved that she had already dried the breakfast dishes and dusted every knick-knack within reach. (And that was before Kaelyn and Olivia were bathed and dressed in clean play clothes!)

I watched the children play nicely, clean up their messes, and say "please" and "thank you" when they should. They even abided by the new "no running in the house" rule!

Then I listened to the director tell me how much the children listen to her because she has that "sound" in her voice. YaYa explained this phenomenon called "respect" and proceeded to chat about her skill in strategically organizing her daughter's kitchen cabinets - one by one - so not to upset anyone in the household.

Our daughters grow into assured and capable young women, moving in a world we scarcely know.

It seems at times impossible that they could have ever been our babies, our toddlers stomping after butterflies. Our skinny schoolgirls frisking along beside us. That these strong hands once clung to ours. That these confident eyes once sought out reassurance.

Until a day when even the strongest and the wisest find they need to touch the past - and they reach out to us.

And we find all they have ever been is not lost..... or ever will be.

Pam Brown,
b.1928

She explained how difficult it must be for her daughter, Cara, to see another mother, never mind her own mother, filling her shoes while she was busy completing her nursing requirements.

All the while YaYa highlighted the well known facts:

Daughters need their mothers. Always have, always will.

"Heck! What are mothers for? Cara and her family will appreciate my hard work someday! And if they don't, I'll remind them," YaYa said proudly.

I had seen and heard all of this when my mother practically moved in with us to help nurture 'respectful' children in an 'organized' environment. *(And just yesterday, wasn't I one of those children playing in Grammy's den?)*

As I got into my car, I laughed and cried. Simultaneously! I laughed because YaYa was so like my mother, a mother who took her role seriously. A mother to the core! And I cried, because those days (for me) are gone forever.

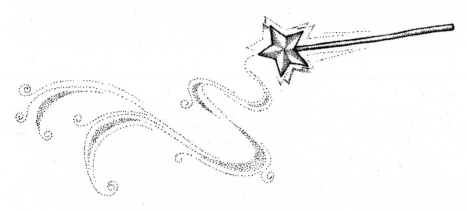

Afterthought:

I'll have to ask YaYa if she carries a whistle in her sweatshirt pocket and refolds her daughter's clean laundry. I bet she does!

Conclusion

My children are busy making an extra large 'play dough pizza'; so with a few quiet minutes I add these final notes.

Parents and children teach each other priceless lessons.

But sometimes those valuable lessons are painful - like we missed out on a whole lot in our former lives.

Every time my kids give me a surprise hug or whisper an unexpected "I love you", I think about all the times my mother yearned to receive those same messages from me.

For so many years I worked hard to build a wall around my heart. That wall was effective for keeping out hurt, but more effective in keeping out love. Learning and loving with my children has helped me to bulldoze that wall. That's probably the best lesson my children have taught me and one of the greatest lessons I want them to learn as well.

Come here girls, so I can give you both a big hug!!

Mom: Good night, Babies. Sleep tight. I love you.
Elizabeth: *I love you more, Mom.*
Jackie: *I love you more than more, Mom. More than the whole world. And more than the sky, and more than the grass, and more than my blankie, and more than the dog, and more than my night light, and more than all lights. More than everything, Mom. Night-night.*
Mom: Goodnight girls.
And then, as if playing one final 'got you last' game for the day, I whisper, LOVE YOU MORE!

My children are not the only children in the world, but they've recreated mine!

Reflection

Despite the day to day challenges of meeting our children's every need, there's nothing more important - or rewarding-than our job as parents.

As a working Mother, I know that parents need support (lots of it) from our family, friends, and the community. Such an intricate and indispensable support system enables us to love our babies, nurture our children, and steer our teens into adulthood.

What responsibility! What challenge! What a community when we coordinate our efforts!

* * *

Okay, I'd say it's high time for a girls' night out. Sorry, not you, Babies, I'm talking to my Sorority Sisters. Let's meet, someplace that doesn't serve Happy Meals or have the word 'monkey' in front of 'bar'.

* * *

Jean Lanahan can be reached at Mommajeana1@aol.com, or at PO Box 406, Sagamore Beach, Massachusetts 02562.

THE END.

ℋbout the Author

Jean Lanahan is mother of two, entrepreneur, and wife of a fisherman. As a team, Jean and her husband, Tom, nurture their children and operate a marina services buisness. Separately, Tom goes fishing; Jean writes in a journal - her place to highlight an enlightening (and demanding) world filled with children.

Before accepting her tenure as 'Momma Jeana', Jean graduated from Aquinas College, Bentley College, and completed (most) of her Business Graduate requirements at Lesley College. Today, the author can be found at her computer, and at playgrounds, drive-through eateries, and libraries. Look for a woman accompanied by children, carrying a notebook or two.

The Lanahan family lives in Sagamore Beach, Massachusetts, and claims to have eaten approximately 10,000 pounds of seafood.

photo by Melissa Elmore

117

Jean Lanahan

𝒜cknowledgements

The author would like to note that declaration of her (and/or her family's) favorite (and/or least favorite) TV shows, movies, songs, books, cleaning products, play places, fish markets, corner stores, animals, teachers, schools, friends, holidays, poems, foods, bugs, toys, bras, boots, watches, riddles, night time stories, vehicles, super heroes, disciplinary tools, fairies -and anything else mentioned in text not listed above - are purely, freedom of speech.

※ ※ ※

The author would like to note that Quotes throughout the book were found in the following places: other books; from the mouths of people she knows; on the internet; or they miraculously appeared on her computer screen.

※ ※ ※

In chronological order, following are published works highlighted in this writing:

Maria Shriver, 1999, *What's Heaven?*, St. Martin's Press, New York

Anonymous Poem, as it appears in *The Greatest Gifts Our Children Give to Us, Steven W. Vannoy. (N.Y.: Simon and Schuster, 1995)*

Robert Munsch, *Love You Forever*, Firefly Books, Ontario; New York, 66th printing, 2003

Loretta Laroche column, "Get A Life: You Can Teach An Old Dog New Tricks", *The Patriot Ledger*, Monday October, 21, 2002

Erma Bombeck, *"No More Oatmeal Kisses"* from *Forever Erma,* Andrews and McMeel, Kansas City, Missouri, 1996

Poem by Pam Brown from *In Praise and Celebration of Daughters, Selected for Hallmark by Helen Exley;* Exley Publications, New York, NY 1997, 2001

Printed in the United States
38833LVS00006B/136-204